The Dukan Diet Life Plan

Dr Pierre Dukan

HODDER &
STOUGHTON

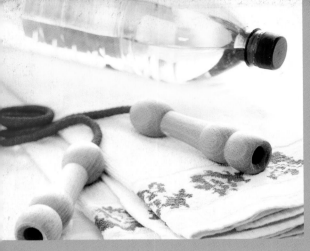

Contents

Introduction   4

A tried-and-tested method

The story behind this diet   8

Carbohydrates, lipids (fats) and proteins   10

What proteins do
(backed up by scientific evidence)   12

The Dukan Diet   14

The diet's four phases   16

Oat bran   18

→ Questions and answers   20

→ In a nutshell...the Dukan method in
twelve key points   22

Phase 1: Attack

What you are aiming for in Phase 1   26

The rules for Phase 1   28

Pure proteins   30

The 72 foods allowed in Attack   32

What can you eat in Phase 1?   38

Breakfast   42

Lunch   44

Dinner   46

Some sample menus for Phase 1 (Attack)   48

Fitting your diet into your daily life (Phase 1)   50

→ Questions and answers   52

→ Phase 1 summary   55

→ The Attack phase in a nutshell   56

Phase 2: Cruise

What you are aiming for in Phase 2	61
The rules for Phase 2	62
Alternating proteins and vegetables	64
What can you eat in Phase 2?	67
How should you prepare vegetables?	68
Prescribed physical exercise	70
Some sample menus for Phase 2 (Cruise)	74
Fitting your diet into your daily life (Phase 2)	76
→ Questions and answers	78
→ Phase 2 summary	80
→ The Cruise phase in a nutshell	82

Phase 3: Consolidation

What you are aiming for in Phase 3	86
The rules for Phase 3	88
What can you eat in Phase 3?	92
Managing celebration meals	94
Pure protein Thursdays	96
Some sample menus for Phase 3 (Consolidation)	98
Fitting your diet into your daily life (Phase 3)	100
→ Questions and answers	102
→ Phase 3 summary	104
→ The Consolidation phase in a nutshell	106

Phase 4: Permanent Stabilization

What you are aiming for in Phase 4	110
The three rules you have to keep to for a very long time	112
Should I opt for foods with reduced fat and sugar?	113
Protein Thursdays	114
What can you eat on protein Thursdays?	116
Some sample menus for Phase 4 (Stabilization)	118
Fitting your protein Thursdays into your daily life (Phase 4)	120
→ Questions and answers	122
→ Phase 4 summary	124
→ The Stabilization phase in a nutshell	126
Two majors advances that change everything: personalization and monitoring	128
Starters and appetizers	**131**
Main courses	**171**
Desserts	**213**
Index	254
Acknowledgements	255

Introduction

For the past thirty-five years, every day in my work as a doctor I have been fighting weight problems. Starting out on my own, I first crafted my skills by working with individual patients in consultations. While still a very young doctor, I was therefore fortunate to devise the protein diet. As the years went by, I improved it, adjusting it based on my patients' feedback and needs. Gradually the diet turned into a comprehensive programme, which was published in France in 2001 entitled *Je Ne Sais Pas Maigrir* (I can't lose weight). Since then, and giving me the greatest rewards imaginable, more than a million people in over twenty countries have read this book. Unfortunately, I do not know how many have followed the diet suggested and, even less, how many have attained their True Weight, consolidated it and, most importantly, never put any weight back on.

However, I do know that every morning I receive an ever-growing number of heartfelt messages from readers who, because they have lost weight using this book and its method, go out of their way to let other people know about it. My method spread simply by word of mouth, without any advertising to back it up. Nowadays, I am conscious that I am no longer the sole owner of my method; it also belongs to all my readers who follow it and recommend it to others.

Who are they? Mostly they are well-organized women, writing from all four corners of the internet world. To date, over 250 sites, forums and blogs have been listed where anonymous contributors and volunteers share their experiences of controlling their weight with my diet. It was these women who eventually named my method after me. I would never have dared do that myself.

This book and method are aimed at people who want to lose weight but, faced with the overwhelming choice of diets available, they do not know how to choose and which one to choose. According to my records, there have been 210 diets since the 1950s, of which 72 have been published. Only 15 have any coherence and they can be boiled down to 7 main programmes:

- **The low-calorie diet** is the oldest and, in theory, the most logical, but in practice the least effective diet.
- **Atkins** was revolutionary and effective, but it leaves the door wide open to fats and cholesterol.
- **Montignac** was Atkins' first successor, with its pros and cons.
- **Weight Watchers'** meetings were very innovative, but its low-calorie diet does it a disservice.
- **The South Beach diet** is a good diet, but it lacks any proper stabilization.
- **The protein powder diet** is the most widely sold throughout the world, but the most unnatural diet. Once dieting is over, it leads to a massive and permanent weight explosion.
- **The method that I suggest.**

I have trouble writing this as it may appear immodest, but I really do believe that, to date, of all the diets put forward my method is by far the best. It is set out simply; it provides a solid framework; it is effective; you start getting immediate results and these results last. Its 100 as-much-as-you-want foods are all natural foods and this concept is simple; it is easy to follow and it can tackle all weight-loss situations. For all these reasons, it seems to me to be the best way we have at the moment of losing weight and, most importantly, of not putting weight back on again.

I am campaigning for this method to become a standard benchmark in the worldwide fight against weight problems. Readers, I am asking you to judge how well it works. In this book, you will find my whole method, along with an introduction to physical exercise, which I now prescribe as I would medication and a recipe section so that during your diet you can keep varying your meals. Recipes provide pleasure and without pleasure our struggle against weight problems would be about restriction and nothing else.

So go off to do battle with these three pointers to encourage you: as much as you want; fast results; enjoy your food!

Are you up for it? Let yourself be guided – your scales are quaking already!

A tried-and-tested
method

What is the only food group that, low in calories, also leaves the body full and satisfied without making it feel tired? Proteins.

The story
behind this diet

It all started when I was a young general practitioner working in Montparnasse in Paris. One of my patients was obese and he seemed to have come to terms with it. However, one day he booked an appointment and asked me to make him lose weight. At first I replied that I was not a specialist in the field. He countered straightaway that he knew all the specialists I was referring to very well and that he had tested all the existing methods without ever managing to lose any weight for any length of time.

Sounding deeply disheartened he told me, 'Since my teens I have lost about 50 stone and as you can see I have put it all back on again!' Then he added, 'I'll follow your instructions to the letter. I'll do whatever you want except for one thing – don't stop me eating meat. I just love meat too much!'

When I immediately shot back the reply, 'Alright, eat only meat, as much meat as you want for five days,' that was how the adventure started.

The following week, my patient was back in my surgery, but this time he was beaming all over his face. He had lost almost 11 pounds!

So we both agreed to continue with the experiment. However, I did ask him to ensure he was drinking enough water and to have a blood test because I was worried about his cholesterol. One week later, his blood tests results were absolutely fine and he had lost another 4 pounds…

I then started studying in greater detail how proteins could usefully contribute to a weight-loss diet. After twenty days of dieting, my patient had lost over a stone and a half, but he was now beginning to grow weary of his favourite food. So we added a few vegetables to his meals, along with some dairy products, eggs and fish. As for quantities, I continued to avoid any restriction. He greatly enjoyed this freedom and, at the same time, he graciously stuck to my very precise instructions about eating only proteins and a few vegetables.

Since then, as you will see from reading these pages, the method has been fine-tuned thanks to feedback from my patients and I have created some simple, easy recipes. However, the basis of the diet has not changed – by eating animal proteins it is possible to lose weight quickly, permanently and without restricting quantity.

With the advent of the internet, I really can combine my experience with that of my patients. The people surfing on my site share their experiences with me; my tips merge with their tips and the women writing on the forums add their own recipes, less professional but just as creative, to my recipes. We work together towards a common goal, which is to lose weight whilst enjoying eating! This book is therefore the end product of many long years of experiments, tests and developments that you can benefit from today.

If, like my first patient, you follow to the letter the instructions that follow, it will be impossible for you not to lose weight quickly. You do not need any complex equipment, just some bathroom scales. You don't need to work out calories, weigh out food or use any tables with complicated figures.

Reading about the different stages of the diet is very easy as you only have two or three instructions to memorize. As for everything else, within this simple structure, you can eat as much as you want.

However, before we start examining the principles behind the diet itself, we need to quickly remind ourselves about the different food groups so that you avoid making mistakes when selecting your ingredients.

Carbohydrates, lipids (fats) and proteins

All the different foods we eat are made up of just three categories of nutrients: carbohydrates, lipids (fats) and proteins. The calorific value of these three groups is different. However, we know today that it is important not to judge a food solely by the number of calories it provides, since the body does not deal with the 100 calories contained in a piece of chocolate cake, fish or a salad dressing in the same way. How many of these calories the body ends up extracting varies greatly, depending on where they come from. This is why it is important to have a sound knowledge of these nutrients so that you can make the right choices with the diet we are going to start together.

Carbohydrates

Carbohydrates can be divided into 'fast sugars' and 'slow sugars'. Fast sugars are the sugars found in sweet-tasting foods such as confectionery, cakes, wine, honey, fruit and so on. Everyone knows that the dieter must avoid them, especially since soon after assimilating fast sugars we feel really hungry again. Bread and pasta as well as pulses such as lentils and dried beans contain slow sugars. These are called slow sugars because the body takes longer to assimilate them than fast sugars. As far as our metabolism goes, fast sugars encourage insulin secretion, which in turn makes the body produce and store fats.

Carbohydrates only provide 4 calories per gram, but we tend to eat them in considerable quantities to feel full.

Until you reach your desired weight, your True Weight, our diet programme cuts out carbohydrates altogether. They will be reintroduced during the Consolidation period (Phase 3). Then during Stabilization (Phase 4), you will be completely free to eat them again six days out of seven.

Lipids (fats)

Dieters usually recognize lipids as their number one enemy if they are hankering after a slim figure. Providing 9 calories per gram, lipids are also known as fats and are virtually absent from our programme. Fats can come from animals and cooked meats contain a lot of fat, as do mutton and lamb. Some poultry and fish are also very fatty, for example duck, goose, salmon, tuna etc. Butter and cream, of course, contain over 80% fat.

Although vegetable fats such as olive or rapeseed oil are beneficial for your health (they are particularly rich in omega fatty acids and good for your heart), they will also be banned throughout your diet, except for up to a teaspoon for a vinaigrette mixture for several people or three drops of oil to grease a pan.

Proteins

Animal products are the most abundant source of protein, meat being extremely rich in it. Some protein foods have hardly any fat at all and are therefore particularly useful in our diet, for example lean cuts of beef, turkey, certain offal, white fish, prawns, crab and so on.

Egg white is the best source of protein and, what's more, it has no cholesterol. You can create a never-ending range of tasty, filling recipes using egg whites.

Cereals and legumes also contain proteins, but these proteins have too many carbohydrates, which is why they are not included in our diet. During the Attack phase, your menus must be made up of proteins, and only proteins.

Proteins – a vital nutrient

It is not dangerous to eat only proteins as part of a diet, quite the opposite in fact, since proteins form the only group of nutrients that your body cannot synthesize on its own. By drawing upon its reserves, your body will find the carbohydrates and lipids (fats) it needs for energy. However, it is incapable of making proteins itself, which is why a diet lacking in proteins may be dangerous. Whenever there is a shortage, the body takes the proteins it needs for its survival from its muscles, skin and even its bones. A diet must therefore always provide at least 1 gram of protein per day for every kilogram of body weight and proteins should be evenly distributed over the day's three meals.

What proteins do
(backed up by scientific evidence)

Pure proteins reduce your appetite

Since proteins are not easily digested, they are powerful appetite suppressants. Indeed, eating a good amount of pure proteins makes your body secrete ketones, which will give you a lasting feeling of satiety. After three days of eating pure proteins, hunger disappears completely. As you are no longer racked by hunger, you can resist snacking more easily.

Eating pure proteins cuts down your calorie intake

For human beings, the ideal proportion for nutrients (enabling us to extract as many calories as possible for our survival) is the following formula: five parts carbohydrates and three parts lipids (fats) to two parts proteins. When our food intake matches this ratio, this is ideal for assimilating nutrients and they are assimilated through the small intestine with maximum efficiency. Once these proportions are reversed, the way the body absorbs its calories is also disrupted, which can be put to particularly good use as part of a diet. Limiting what we eat to just one of the three food groups, automatically results in calories being less well absorbed. However, eating only carbohydrates or lipids (fats) is inconceivable as it would endanger your health in the long term by increasing cholesterol and causing diabetes and cardiovascular complaints. A diet based on a single food group without putting your body at risk is only possible with proteins. Give your digestive system protein meals and it will struggle to extract all the calories contained in the food. So the body will then attempt to take only the proteins it absolutely needs to maintain its organs, making very little use of the remaining calories available.

Pure proteins help you combat water retention

Diets based on plants, fruits, vegetables and mineral salts encourage water retention. The diet that you are going to try, based on proteins, is quite the opposite. It is water-repellent, promoting the elimination of

By digesting proteins you burn up calories!

Digesting proteins is an extremely lengthy process. Did you know that it takes over three hours to digest and assimilate a high-protein meal? But this is not all; in order to extract calories from proteins, the body has to work very hard indeed. It has been calculated that to get 100 calories, 30 of them are used up! Just having to digest a high-protein meal reduces the calories it provides.

urine, which is especially useful during the menopause or if you are simply premenstrual. Our programme is therefore very beneficial for women who tend to retain water more easily in their tissues. Some of my female patients, with little experience of being overweight before the menopause, unexpectedly find themselves with swollen ankles, heavy legs and a bloated stomach. All of a sudden, the odd bit of dieting they had tended to rely on throughout their lives (for example, eating carefully after a week of festivities) no longer has any effect. Our diet's Attack phase, with proteins and nothing else, works miracles for them.

Proteins are an effective way of tackling cellulite

The results of a high-protein diet on cellulite are quite spectacular. Quite simply, these results can be explained by the water-repellent effect of proteins and the intense filtering of the kidneys. Water goes into tissues and comes out again full of waste matter. The cellulite is cleaned out. This is why, and we will keep on saying it, drinking lots of water throughout the diet is crucial.

Remember to drink lots of water to get rid of waste

The body uses just some of the proteins it is given. Only about 50% can be assimilated, the rest is eliminated as waste in your urine and may lead to an increase in uric acid. To offset this minor inconvenience, all you need do is make sure that you drink enough throughout the diet (1.5–2 litres of water per day). Our studies show that if sufficient water is drunk, eating proteins poses no particular risk. This proteins + water combination is even very beneficial in flushing out cellulite!

The **Dukan** Diet

How does the diet work?

The diet is made up of a 'diet duo' that works like a two-stroke engine. A pure protein diet period, the Attack diet, is followed by a period of proteins combined with vegetables, the Cruise diet, allowing the body the time it needs to recuperate and digest its weight loss. This is the basis of the Dukan Diet.

However, with the experience I gained from treating my patients, I realized that this two-pronged attack was not quite enough. Once they had lost weight and reached their goal, my patients actually showed a great propensity for just letting everything go and would quickly put back on the weight they had lost. This is why the weight-loss diet duo is now part of a much wider programme, made up of four stages that cannot possibly be separated from each other. Please note that you must agree to the whole programme, you either take it or leave. If you skip a phase, one thing is certain – your diet will be doomed to failure.

In return, embracing the diet as a whole offers certain advantages and your motivation is bound to remain riding high, for four reasons:

• The Dukan programme gives you a list of very precise instructions. To succeed, all you have to do is follow them.
• The Dukan programme is a completely natural diet. Of all the natural diets, it is the one that produces the best results.
• The Dukan programme is not frustrating since there are no limits restricting the quantities you can eat.
• You cannot follow the Dukan programme half-heartedly. Either you succeed and agree to everything or you fail!

The four main stages in the Dukan programme

•Phase 1: Attack phase (pure proteins)

This Attack phase in your diet contains only pure proteins. It gets underway with lightning speed and the weight loss is very quick.

•Phase 2: Cruise phase (proteins + vegetables)

After this initial period when you have started to wage war on your surplus pounds, there then follows a 'Cruise' period, during which you opt for a diet of alternating days of pure proteins and vegetables and proteins. This way you will reach your chosen weight.

•Phase 3: Consolidation phase

Once you have got down to the weight you wanted, it is important to avoid the rebound phenomenon – after rapid weight loss, the body tends to pile back on any lost pounds extremely quickly. This is therefore an especially tricky period and under no circumstances is the diet over yet. For every pound you have lost, you will need to remain five days in the Consolidation phase.

•Phase 4: Stabilization phase

The permanent Stabilization period is every bit as crucial because it is decisive in determining the success of your diet. So that you do not put back on any of the weight you have lost, you will have to apply some simple measures throughout your life. One day a week you must follow the Dukan Diet's Attack phase to the letter, preferably every Thursday. Having to do this will protect you from regaining weight.

As you can see, the Dukan programme takes care of you so that you are never ever left to cope on your own again.

The diet's
four phases

PHASE 1
The Attack phase with pure proteins (PP)

This is the most motivating period as you will see your scales drop with breathtaking speed, a little as if you were fasting. This Attack phase is a real machine of war.

During this phase you are going to eat the purest possible proteins, whilst cutting out all other foods as much as possible. In reality, it is not possible to eliminate carbohydrates and fats altogether from what you eat. In fact, apart from egg whites, no food is made up entirely of protein. Therefore your diet will bring together a certain number of foods whose composition is as close as possible to pure protein including, for example, some categories of meat, fish, shellfish, poultry, eggs and fat-free dairy products.

Length: this period can last between one and ten days, depending on how much weight is to be lost.

PHASE 2
The Cruise phase where pure proteins (PP) alternate with proteins/vegetables (PV)

This second phase cannot be separated from the first one as they both work together. You are going to alternate periods of proteins + vegetables with periods of pure proteins.

Just like the first diet, this second one allows you the same complete freedom regarding quantities. Both diets let you eat 'as much as you want' of the foods allowed at any time.

Later on we will look at how you alternate these two diets, which will depend on how much weight you have to lose, your age and also your motivation.

Length: you have to follow this Cruise phase without any breaks until you get down to the weight you want.

PHASE 3
Consolidating the weight you have slimmed down to

The essential purpose of this phase is to get you eating more foods again and to stabilize your weight. You will be able to eat a greater variety of foods, but you need to avoid the rebound effect and the risk of regaining weight. Your body will try to resist, even more so if you have just lost a considerable amount of weight. Given that its reserves have been plundered, your body will now react by attempting to store up some new reserves. To do this, it will cut down as far as possible the amount of energy it uses and it will absorb as much as it can from any food you eat. During this period, a copious meal that would have had little impact at the start of the diet will now have far-reaching repercussions.

This is why the quantities of richer foods will be limited so that, without running any risks, you can wait for your metabolism to calm down and for the rebound effect to subside. This rebound effect is one of the most common reasons why weight-loss diets do not work.

Length: this depends on how much weight has been lost and can be very easily calculated: five days of Consolidation for every pound lost.

PHASE 4
Stabilization forever

We have seen that people who have been overweight realize full well that, even after dieting, they will not manage to eat with the moderation and measure that most nutritionists rightly recommend as being the guaranteed way to keep them at the weight they have slimmed down to. This is why it is important to support someone who has just finished their Consolidation phase, bearing in mind that their personality is that of a person who used to be 'fat'.

In this fourth phase, the diet requires you to eat the initial Attack diet one day a week (usually on Thursdays).

Length: for as long as possible, even better, for the rest of your life. By following the few measures in Phase 4, you will be able to eat like everyone else without putting any weight back on.

A diet that includes lots of water

It is important to drink at least 1.5 litres of water per day because once proteins are digested, waste products get into the body in the form of uric acid. Moreover, if you drink water this diet works better because although losing weight is about burning up calories, it is also about eliminating waste. Just like any other combustion process, the energy burnt up when you diet produces waste products and these have to be got rid off. Not only does not drinking enough slow down your weight loss, it can also be toxic for your body.

A low-salt diet

The Dukan Diet is water-repellent, so it fights water retention effectively. Eating food that is too salty will keep the water in your tissues. Remember that 1 litre of water weighs 1kg and it only takes 9g of salt for your tissues to store 1 litre of water!

Oat bran

The Dukan Diet is also based on an outstanding foodstuff: oat bran. To my mind, oat bran is the best food there is for protecting our health.

Oat bran gently improves digestion

In nature there are two types of fibre: soluble fibre, found in the pectin in apples and oat bran, and insoluble fibre. Insoluble fibre, like the fibre in wheat bran, can be very irritating for sensitive bowels, whereas soluble fibre is far kinder. Soluble fibre turns into a sort of gel and eases digestion, while at the same time taking away with it a few of the calories from the food eaten. Eaten daily, oat bran will help you keep your figure – 'little brooks make great rivers'. For anyone who is very sensitive to oat bran and reacts to it, you can still eat bran if you soften it up by soaking it in some milk for half an hour.

Oat bran is satisfying

When it comes into contact with water, oat bran swells up and occupies twenty to thirty times its volume in the stomach. So the stomach feels full and is kept busy for a long time.

Oat bran is slimming

Oat bran has this extraordinary ability to trap calories in the small intestine and take them away with it into the stools. You will not lose many calories, but as you lose them repeatedly and over time, this adds up to a significant amount. Furthermore, digestion often slows down during dieting and oat bran eases it as much as possible, but without forcing it.

Oat bran reduces cholesterol levels

Many studies have already shown how important fibre is in controlling cholesterol and oat bran is by far the fibre that has the most impact on cholesterol levels in the blood. Eaten as part of a balanced diet, oat bran reduces cholesterol levels considerably. Eating oat bran is recommended to help prevent cardiovascular diseases.

Oat bran protects you from diabetes

By slowing down the rate at which fast sugars are absorbed into the blood, oat bran also reduces insulin secretion and prevents the pancreas from becoming overworked.

Oat bran protects you from cancer of the colon

If you eat oat bran every day and drink lots of water, oat bran protects the lining of the intestine. Our intestine is a filter, and this filter can get clogged up from pollution, an unbalanced diet, pesticides, food intolerances and so on. The lining of the intestine may also become irritated. Oat bran works like an intestinal sponge in that it absorbs and cleans, as long as it is eaten every day.

Can you eat several doses of oat bran per day?

During the actual weight-loss period (the Attack phase and then the Cruise phase until you attain your True Weight), you should ideally not exceed 2 tablespoonfuls of bran per day.

• 1 tablespoonful per day is not just allowed – it is recommended.

• 2 tablespoonfuls slightly increase the bran's impact and ease your bowel movements.

• 3 tablespoonfuls further improve digestion and bowel movements, but start to provide calories. As soon as you go into Stabilization (Phase 4), you can step up to this daily dose of 3 tablespoonfuls.

Questions and answers

Should I ask my doctor to monitor me whilst on the Dukan Diet?

→ If you are under 50 and in sound health, if you have no ongoing medical complaints, no cardiac or renal risk factors, if you are not depressive, insulin-dependent, anorexic or bulimic, there is absolutely no reason to worry, especially if you make full use of one of the best things about the Dukan Diet: you can freely eat vegetables and high-protein foods once you have reached phase 2.

→ Once you are over 50, it is a good idea for your doctor to give you a general examination and to have tests done in case a lazy thyroid shows up or there are hormonal problems with water retention.

→ Ideally your doctor will know you well enough to be able to help you follow your diet properly, take your blood pressure and work out your blood test results. Losing weight is a difficult enterprise that goes against our nature, so any help is welcome and invaluable.

Can I use protein bars and powders?

This is not possible for two reasons:

→ Most of the bars sold in shops are high in carbohydrates and, compared with what is recommended in this diet, their protein content is far too low. Whenever you cannot cook, go for food that is easy to eat such as cooked chicken or turkey slices and seafood sticks. You can also stock up your fridge with fat-free fromage frais and yoghurts.

→ Only synthetic powdered proteins contain enough protein, but our programme works with real, natural proteins and not with powdered ones. In the Stabilization phase, and only as a stopgap, you may use powdered proteins that contain at least 95% protein.

How can I diet and watch my cholesterol?

→ You just have to be particularly careful with eggs. If your cholesterol is not worrying, you can have one whole egg per day. If your cholesterol level is a little too high, then cook just with egg whites. If this is the case, make your oat bran galette using only the egg white (see the recipe on page 42). Otherwise, eat as many egg whites as you want, but limit yourself to four yolks per week.

I tend to skip meals – will this speed up my diet?

→ Quite the opposite. You must make sure that you never skip meals as it is completely counterproductive and should be avoided at all costs! If, for example, you skip lunch, the chances are that by five o'clock you will be ravenous at a time when, no doubt, you will feel like devouring a bar of chocolate. However, let's imagine that you manage to hold on until dinner. You are then bound to eat more and choose more comforting foods – starchy foods, bread, fatty products and so on. And your body is going to penalize you too by extracting as much as it can from whatever you feed it with. From what you eat at each meal, the body extracts a reasonable amount from the food. Let's say that it takes 70 to 75%. If you skip lunch, not only will you then eat more at the next meal, but your body will extract up to 95%. So you end up losing out on all fronts.

In a nutshell...**the Dukan method in twelve key points**

1 Effectiveness
I know of nobody who, having followed the method with motivation and confidence, has not lost weight, attained their True Weight, then consolidated and stabilized it.

2 It works quickly
With the Attack, the method gets going with lightning speed, maintaining, and even increasing, motivation tenfold.

3 Simplicity
100 foods, 72 proteins, 28 vegetables.

4 No hunger
The 100 foods come with the magic words, 'as much as you want'.

5 A clear structure based on four phases
Precise and clear guidance on which to lean.
A non-negotiable road map from which it is hard to deviate.

6 Each person has their True Weight
This concept enables every overweight person who is about to start dieting to calculate what their correct weight should be. Your True Weight is an 'attainable and maintainable' weight.

7 A natural method
The 100 foods in my method are
fundamentally human. These are foods that we
have always eaten, the 'hunter-gatherers' foods'.

8 A stabilization contract
Three simple, concrete
measures, prescribed for life.

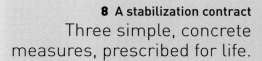

9 A didactic programme
Lose weight while learning to lose weight by
instinctively understanding the importance of
foods according to the order they are introduced.

10 The PE concept
'Prescribed exercise' is a radically new way of
prescribing the second driving force behind weight
loss, just like medication.

11 The method now includes personalization
A weight-loss programme stands a much better chance of
succeeding if it is personalized. With the internet, this is now
possible (see page 128).

12 The method now includes online monitoring and coaching
Monitoring, day after day, pound after pound, is finally available
on the net, where the method has become interactive through
the exchange of morning instructions and the user's evening
reports (see page 129).

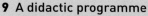

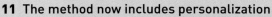

Phase 1: **Attack**

The pure proteins phase gets the diet off to a lightning start. Once you are following it, you are in control of a mighty bulldozer that will crush all resistance in its path. So get on board!

What you are aiming
for in Phase 1

Just one instruction to follow: you can eat as much as you want of the foods that are allowed

In the following pages, you will find a list of foods you are allowed to eat (see page 38). They are yours and you can eat as much of them as you want. As for other foods, forget about them for the time being.

Make sure you drink at least 1.5 litres of water per day. By drinking more, you will feel as if there is 'something there' and you will also feel full more quickly. You may need to go to the loo a lot as not being used to drinking so much, your kidneys are forced to open their valves and eliminate. Very soon, you'll seem so much lighter, your face will be thinner and rings will slip off as your fingers are no longer swollen!

Getting through the first three days

The Attack diet uses the surprise effect: your body will just have to get used to a new way of eating.

• The first day on this Attack diet

This is a day of adjustment and combat. Of course the door is wide open to many categories of common and tasty foods, but it is closed to many others that you are used to eating. To get your diet started, try and choose a day when you can relax and are free to feed yourself as you want. The start of a weekend may be ideal, but you decide, depending on how your week is structured.

During these first three days you will feel very restricted. To remedy this and stay on course, make sure you fill your fridge with the foods you are allowed. Then you can take full advantage of what this diet offers as, for the first time, you can eat 'as much as you want' of foods as dense and prized as beef, veal, fish and shellfish of every kind (including smoked salmon, tinned tuna, smoked haddock, seafood sticks (surimi), oysters and prawns) as well as scrambled eggs, the endless variety of low-fat dairy products and low-fat sliced meats – the choice is yours! So on the first day, eat more. Make up for what you cannot eat with the quantity of what you can have.

• **The second day**

During these first two days you might feel a little tired and less inclined to any prolonged effort. Your body has been 'taken by surprise' during the Attack diet and it is burning up calories without counting or resisting, so this is not the right time to put it through an intense workout. During this period avoid hard, physical exercise and extreme sports.

• **From the third day onwards**

Your tiredness will go and it is usually replaced by a sense of euphoria and dynamic energy that are further reinforced by the encouraging message on your scales. Your hunger also disappears. This surprising disappearance is due to ketone bodies being released, the most powerful natural appetite suppressants. It may also be caused by weariness in anyone who is not a great meat- and fish-eater – monotony has a marked effect on appetite. After this third day, raging hunger and cravings for sweet things disappear.

A decisive weight loss

A real psychological turning point and surprise for your metabolism, this Attack phase should enable you to lose, quickly and effectively, as much weight as your body can lose during this short length of time. You will be surprised by it.

A solution for constipation

Constipation comes about because protein foods contain very little fibre. Buy some oat bran and add it to your yoghurts. Most importantly, drink as much as you are meant to. In addition to the well-known fact that water makes you urinate, drinking also adds water to your stools. This softens them and makes it much easier for them to pass through the system, which eases digestion.

Your mouth feels dry

Having a dry mouth and bad breath are symptoms that occur with any weight-loss diet and will be a little more noticeable here than they might be with more gradual diets. These symptoms are therefore a sign that you are indeed losing weight and so you should welcome them as proof of your success. To ease them, you should drink more and use sugar-free chewing gum.

Three meals a day

Even if the principle of this diet is based on you being able to eat as much as you want of the foods on the list we give you, nonetheless, it is important to stick to a normal eating pattern with three meals. First and foremost, if you skip a meal your body will 'take revenge' at the next meal. You are likely to cave in to foods that are not allowed and your body, which by definition dislikes any frustration, will hoard even more from the foods you do give it.

Weigh yourself!

During the Attack phase, keep on weighing yourself because this will keep you in good spirits as, hour by hour, you see your scales veer in the right direction. Your scales are your friend. They will give you encouragement during the Attack and Cruise phases and help you to remain vigilant during the Consolidation and Stabilization phases.

The rules for
Phase 1

How long?

The Attack diet consists of pure proteins. How long this stage lasts will vary according to your age, how much weight you have to lose and how many diets you have previously tried. Here are a few ideas to help you set your target clearly and stick to it.

• To lose under 10 pounds

You are recommended to avoid an all-too-rapid start – a single day may be enough. This first day, the opening day, has the advantage of providing a complete break with the past that takes your body by surprise, producing an astonishing weight loss that is enough to encourage you to get going with the diet.

• To lose under 20 pounds

I would suggest you start with a three-day Attack diet, which will allow you to proceed effortlessly to the alternating proteins phase.

• To lose between 20 and 40 pounds

To lose this amount, the Attack diet should last five days. This is the length of time needed to allow the diet to provide the best results without your metabolism developing resistance or you growing weary of it. This is usually how long this Attack phase lasts.

• To lose over 40 pounds

With major obesity, when a person wants to lose over 40 pounds, it is possible, after taking medical advice, to carry on with the pure proteins phase for up to seven, and even ten, days. You may also opt for this time period (after talking to your doctor) if you have previously tried lots of diets, as your body is very likely to be stubbornly resistant. In this case, it is absolutely essential that you drink at least 1.5 litres of water per day.

How do you keep on course?

• Read, and keep reading, your list of allowed foods very carefully, drawing up a shopping list for the ones you enjoy eating. Don't just rely on this list, but follow the instructions that can be summed up in just a few words: lean meat, fish and shellfish, poultry, sliced cooked meats, eggs, fat-free dairy products and water.

• Eat as often as you want. The diet allows quantity, so make the most of this!

• Never skip a meal as this would be a serious mistake. You will eat more at the next meal or, even worse, give in and eat foods you are not allowed. And your body will make you pay dearly for this extra restriction.

• Drink a lot and drink every time you eat. To get rid of waste properly, you absolutely must drink at least 1.5 litres of water per day. Water will also help you feel replete.

• Fill up your fridge! If you should happen to run out of proteins and feel hungry, you are going to binge on some food you are not allowed. Make sure that you shop regularly so that you do not have to go without.

When will it be difficult?

The first three days may be a tricky time as your body is going to have to get used to this new way of eating.

You will have to get the better of your hunger, which will fade away from the third day onwards. And you are going to feel constipated, but the oat bran will soon sort this out.

You may also find that during the first three days you have an intense longing for sweet things. Hold firm, three days is not the end of the world. If you manage to stay the course, your hunger, as well compulsive cravings for sugar, will disappear as your diet evolves.

Pure proteins

What are they?

Of all the foodstuffs we eat, only egg white is made up of virtually pure proteins. However, there are a certain number of foods that come close to the perfection we are seeking, which is why you will find the following proteins (all extremely rich in pure proteins) on the list of foods allowed during this first phase:

- beef (but not rib-eye steak, rib of beef or any cuts for stewing)
- veal
- poultry (except for duck and goose)
- fish
- shellfish
- eggs
- fat-free dairy products

The law of all or nothing

How effective this Phase 1 is will depend entirely on the foods selected. The diet will work with lightning speed provided you eat only from this category of foods. But be careful, if you do not follow this instruction to the letter, your diet will be slowed down, even blocked or ruined. So you must not allow yourself any extras whatsoever. To you a tiny square of chocolate after your grilled meat may appear harmless, but for your body it changes everything. As we have explained earlier, the principle of the diet is based on your body having to digest proteins and nothing else. If you introduce sugars or fats into your day, your protein fasting will be compromised.

It is impossible, therefore, to follow this diet half-heartedly. The Dukan Diet obeys the law of all or nothing. If you decide to follow it 'a little', its metabolic effectiveness will be put in jeopardy.

On the other hand, if you stick to this single instruction without deviation, your diet will drive your body to:

- burn up calories to digest the proteins;
- digest the protein foods more slowly;
- very quickly draw on its reserves without diminishing either your

muscles or your bones;
- eliminate waste and get rid of cellulite;
- fight against oedema and water retention;
- reduce its appetite.

Take heart, this stage does not last very long, so hold on tight and keep going!

An ideal diet to tackle water retention

You can also use the pure proteins phase if at times in your life you feel that you are putting on a pound or two here and there. Two or three days of pure proteins can put your body back on track again. This comment is aimed in particular at those women who feel 'bloated' at the end of their menstrual cycle and at women who, around the age of fifty, start noticing their body change even though they are not eating any more than usual. How and why women put on weight happens to be more complex than it is for men and is often linked with water retention. A few days of pure proteins will mean you no longer feel 'bloated' and this phase in the diet is really good at dealing with the feeling of heavy legs and podgy fingers etc. In addition to the results displayed on your scales, you will rediscover your real shape and your figure will be transformed.

After following your diet, you will be able to enjoy all the beneficial effects of Phase 1 throughout your life thanks to the protein Thursdays that we will introduce in the Stabilization phase.

Gaining weight in the menopause

Obviously, the menopause is a very tricky time in a woman's life as far as weight is concerned, but we must not throw in the towel. As soon as the first few pounds start to take hold, it is important to act. If this happens, one protein Thursday per week or two days every fortnight may be enough to keep you at your ideal weight. As for the other days, avoid drinking too much water and go easy with the salt so that you limit water retention. Whilst we are on this subject, stop eating ready-made meals as they alone are responsible for almost 90% of the salt we consume!

The 72 foods allowed in Attack

Always have to hand or in your fridge a wide selection from the food categories that are going to become your friends and your best-loved foods. When you are out and about take them with you as most protein foods require some preparation and, unlike carbohydrates and fats, do not keep as well and cannot be found as easily as biscuits and chocolate in drawers and cupboards.

Before you eat a food, make sure that it appears on the list on page 38. Never be without the foods you need for your diet. To be really sure of what you are doing, keep this list with you during the first week. It is simple and boils down to just a few words: lean meats and offal, fish and shellfish, poultry, sliced cooked meats and eggs, fat-free dairy products and drinks.

Lean meats

• Beef

All cuts for roasting or grilling are allowed, in particular steaks, fillet, sirloin, roast beef and other prime, lean cuts.

• Minced steak

Uncooked minced steak can be prepared tartare- or carpaccio-style, but without any oil. It can also be mixed with an egg, some herbs and capers, shaped into meatballs and cooked in the oven.

Minced beef is allowed, but make sure that the fat content does not exceed 10%, as 15% fat is too rich for the Attack period.

• Veal

Veal escalopes and roast veal are recommended. Veal chops are allowed as long as all the surrounding fat is cut off.

How should I cook my meat?

Meats should be prepared without using any fat, butter, oil or cream, even if it is low-fat. You are advised to grill your meat, but these meats can also be roasted in the oven or a rotisserie, cooked in foil parcels or even boiled. How much you cook them is left to each individual's personal preference, but remember that cooking gradually removes the fat from the meat, bringing it closer to the ideal pure protein state that underlies this diet. Go ahead and use spices to avoid monotony.

• **Rabbit**

A source of lean meat that can be eaten roasted or cooked with mustard and fat-free fromage frais.

Offal

You may eat calf's and lamb's tongue as well as liver. Liver contains many vitamins, which are extremely useful during a weight-loss diet. However, it does contain cholesterol, so if you have cholesterol problems, eat it in moderation.

Fish

There is no restriction or limitation with this family of foods. All fish are allowed, whether they are lean or fatty, white or oily, fresh or frozen, tinned in brine or water (not in oil), smoked or dried.

• **All fatty and oily fish**

They are all allowed, in particular sardines, mackerel, tuna and salmon.

• **Smoked fish**

Although smoked salmon looks shiny and greasy, it is hardly any fattier than a 90% fat-free steak. The same goes for smoked trout, eel and haddock.

• **Tinned fish**

Very handy for quick meals or snacks. Tinned fish is allowed if it is in water or brine, like tuna and salmon, or mackerel without its sauce.

• **Seafood sticks (surimi)**

Made from extremely lean white fish, seafood sticks are totally allowed as they are very handy and easy to take around with you.

How should I cook my fish?

Fish should be cooked without adding any fat. Sprinkle it with lemon juice and herbs and spices or bake it in the oven stuffed with herbs and lemon. You can also steam it or, even better, cook it in a foil parcel so that you keep in all the cooking juices.

Shellfish

You may eat as much as you want of prawns, Mediterranean prawns, Dublin Bay prawns, crab, shrimp, cockles, lobster, oysters, mussels and scallops. They will add a festive touch to your diet.

Poultry

All poultry is allowed, except birds with flat beaks such as farm-reared ducks and geese. Be careful not to eat any skin.

• Chicken

Of the different parts, the white meat is the leanest, then choose the legs and lastly the wings.

• Turkey

Acceptable in all forms. Try pan-fried escalopes or a roast drumstick stuffed with garlic.

Low-fat sliced and cooked meats, with any rind cut off

Fine if lean, low-fat and trimmed of all rind. With cooked meat, go for ham or turkey slices as they only have a fat content of between 2% and 4%. They are handy for quick snack lunches.

Eggs

• **Whole eggs**

They can be eaten hard-boiled, soft-boiled, poached or fried, in an omelette or scrambled in a non-stick frying pan, i.e. without adding any oil or butter.

• **Egg white on its own**

Eggs are high in cholesterol and their excessive consumption should be avoided by anyone with an unusually high cholesterol level in their blood. You are recommended to only eat three or four egg yolks a week, whereas the white, a pure protein par excellence, may be eaten without any restriction. If this is the case, it may also be a good idea to make your omelettes and scrambled eggs using one yolk to two whites.

Fat-free dairy products

• **Fat-free plain dairy products**

Yoghurt, fromage frais, quark, cottage cheese – you can eat as much as you want of them.

• **Fat-free flavoured dairy products (vanilla, coconut, lemon and so on)**

You can eat them as much as you want.

• **Low-fat dairy products with fruit, but sugar-free**

In Phase 1 they are tolerated, but it would be better to avoid them. Ideally in Attack you will not eat them, but one, or even two, can be tolerated.

• **Skimmed milk**

Fresh or powdered, it is allowed and can improve the taste and consistency of tea or coffee. Skimmed milk can also be used to make sauces, creams, custards and in a range of other dishes.

What should I drink?

All types of water are allowed, especially spring waters that are slightly diuretic, just as long as they do not contain too much sodium. For older people, it is best to drink water with a high calcium and magnesium content. If you do not care much for still water, you may drink carbonated water as the bubbles and gas have no effect on this diet. However, you should avoid Badoit and San Pellegrino, for example, which are excellent but contain too much sodium for this diet. If you really must, you can have one glass, but no more.

You are allowed to drink diet fizzy drinks (Diet Coke, Coke Zero and other diet drinks).

Remember too that you can drink tea, herbal teas and chicory-based drinks.

Sweeteners

Sugar is not allowed, but you can use aspartame without any restriction. Remember that powdered aspartame loses some of its sweetening power if it is heated, so do not cook with it.

Drinks

It is absolutely vital you drink at least 1.5 litres of liquid per day during your diet. This is not a recommendation, but an obligation. The quantity of liquid is not negotiable, for two reasons:

• Once the body digests the proteins, they release a great amount of waste products into your body in the form of urea. To get rid of these waste products, it is absolutely vital that you drink enough.

• Throughout your diet your body will get rid of stored fat, and water will help your body with this. By drinking copiously, you will be draining it thoroughly.

Even if you are doing everything you should, you will stop losing weight if you do not drink enough. Instead of being flushed out, the waste produced from burning up your fat will accumulate.

Seasonings and condiments

You will find the exhaustive list of the condiments you are allowed on page 41.

• Salt

Salt is allowed, but must be eaten in moderation, especially if you suffer from water retention. If you are experiencing the menopause or premenopause, avoid salt or opt instead for reduced-sodium salts.

• Oil

Although some oils, such as olive oil, are rightly reputed as being good for the heart and arteries, they are nonetheless oils and pure fats and so have no place in this pure protein diet. You can, however, use up to a teaspoon for a vinaigrette mixture for several people or three drops of oil to grease a pan.

• Vinegar

Vinegar is very much a feature of this diet. Choose strong-tasting vinegars such as balsamic and sherry vinegar, but avoid the cheapest ones as some inexpensive balsamic vinegars contain caramel and therefore lots of sugar.

• **Lemon juice**

This can be used to flavour fish and shellfish, but it cannot be consumed as a lemon juice drink or lemonade, even without sugar, because then the lemon is no longer a condiment but a fruit, sour to be sure, but nevertheless a source of sugar and incompatible with pure proteins.

• **Mustard**

Mustard must be eaten in moderation during this Attack phase. There are salt-free mustards if you suffer from water retention.

• **Gherkins and pickled onions**

They are allowed if used as condiments, but cease being part of a pure protein diet if used in such quantities that they have to be considered vegetables.

• **Ordinary ketchup**

This is not allowed as it is both very salty and very sweet. However, there are sugar-free diet ketchups that may be used in moderation.

Seasoning and spices

Thyme, garlic, parsley, onion, shallots, chives and so on, as well as all spices, are not only allowed but are heartily recommended. By using them you can enhance the flavour of the dishes you eat so that the food leaves you feeling replete and satisfied afterwards.

What can you eat in Phase 1?

Meat

Allowed	Not allowed
Beef steak/Minced steak (max. 10% fat content)	Lamb
Fillet of beef	Rib of beef
Sirloin steak	Rib-eye steak
Roast beef	Pork
Rump steak	
Veal escalope/Roast veal	
Veal chop (trimmed of fat)	
Game (venison, pheasant, partridge, grouse)	
Rabbit	

Offal

Allowed	Not allowed
Tongue (calf's and lamb's)	Ox tongue
Kidney	
Calf's liver	

Cooked meats

Allowed	Not allowed
Bresaola (air-dried/wind-dried beef)	Cured ham
Cooked ham slices (no fat/rind)	Smoked ham
Cooked chicken/turkey slices (no fat/rind)	
Fat-reduced bacon	

Fish

Allowed	Not allowed
Cod (fresh)/Ling	Mackerel in sauce
Dab/Lemon sole	Sardines or tuna in oil
Dover sole	
Fish roe (cod, salmon, herring, mullet)	
Grey mullet	
Haddock	
Hake	
Halibut	
Herring	
Mackerel	
Monkfish	
Plaice	
Pollock/Coley	
Rainbow trout/Salmon trout	
Red mullet	
Salmon	
Sardines	
Sea bass	
Sea bream	
Seafood sticks (surimi)	
Skate	
Smoked salmon (and smoked trout, haddock and eel)	
Swordfish	
Tuna (and tinned tuna in water/brine)	
Turbot	
Whiting	

Shellfish

Allowed	Not allowed
Calamari/Squid	
Clams	
Cockles	
Crab	
Crayfish	
Dublin Bay prawns	
Lobster	
Mediterranean prawns/	
Gambas	
Mussels	
Oysters	
Prawns	
Scallops	
Shrimps	
Whelks	

Poultry

Allowed	Not allowed
Chicken (without the skin)	Duck
Chicken livers	Goose
Guinea fowl	
Ostrich	
Pigeon	
Poussin	
Quail	
Turkey	

Eggs

Allowed	Not allowed
Hen's eggs	
Quail's eggs	

Dairy products

Allowed	Not allowed
Fat-free Greek yoghurt/	Cheese
Fat-free natural yoghurt	Whole milk dairy products
(plain or flavoured with	
aspartame)	
Fat-free fromage frais	
Virtually fat-free cottage	
cheese/virtually fat-free	
quark	
Skimmed milk (fresh or	
powdered)	
Extra-light cream cheese	

Vegetable proteins

Allowed	Not allowed
Tofu	

What can you eat in Phase 1?

Condiments

Allowed

Agar-agar
Baking powder
Basil
Cardamom
Chervil
Chilli
Chives
Cinnamon
Cloves
Coriander
Cumin
Garlic
Gelatine (powder/leaves)
Gherkins/Cornichons/
Pickled onions
Ginger
Horseradish
Lemons and limes (except
in drinks)
Lemongrass
Lemon, lime and orange
zest
Low-salt stock cubes
Mint
Nutmeg
Oat bran
Onions/Shallots/Dried
onion
Orange flower water
Paprika
Parsley
Pepper
Rosemary
Saffron
Seaweed
Soy sauce
Star anise
Sugar-free food flavourings
Sweeteners
Tarragon
Teriyaki sauce
Thyme
Turmeric
Vanilla (pods, flavouring
and sugar-free powder)
Vinegars

Tolerated

Dukan mayonnaise
Dukan vinaigrette
Harissa
Mustard
Salt
Stock
Tomato purée (for cooking)
Sugar-free diet ketchup

Not allowed

Butter
Chocolate
Crème fraîche
Dried fruit
Ketchup
Mayonnaise
Nuts
Oils (except for up to 1
teaspoon for a vinaigrette
or to grease a pan)
Olives
Sugar

Oat bran galette recipe

INGREDIENTS
- 1½ tablespoons oat bran
- 1 whole egg or just the white
- 1½ tablespoons fat-free fromage frais or virtually fat-free quark
- 1 teaspoon aspartame or a little salt (according to taste)

Combine the oat bran, egg white or whole egg (depending on your appetite and cholesterol level) with the fromage frais or quark and the sweetener or salt. Mix together thoroughly, then cook the galette in a non-stick frying pan without any fat (if the galette sticks to your pan, you can wipe a drop of oil over the surface using some kitchen paper). If you are suffering from constipation you can also add one teaspoon of wheat bran per day.

Breakfast

What can you eat for breakfast in Phase 1?

You may choose what you want from this list and create a breakfast menu to suit your tastes.

DRINKS

Coffee

Skimmed milk

Tea/Herbal teas

Chicory coffee alternatives

DAIRY PRODUCTS

Virtually fat-free cottage cheese

Fat-free fromage frais

Virtually fat-free quark

Fat-free yoghurt

CRÊPES

Oat bran galette (2 tablespoonfuls oat bran maximum)

MEAT AND EGGS

Cooked chicken (without any fat or rind)

Cooked ham (without any fat or rind)

Cooked turkey (without any fat or rind)

Bresaola

Scrambled, fried, poached or soft-boiled eggs (with chicken breast 'soldiers')

Omelette

If you cannot eat anything when you wake up

You must on no account skip this meal. Have a hot drink, wait an hour, and then have breakfast.

How can I go without bread?

You will have realized that for breakfast there is no deviation from the list of allowed foods, which is why you will not see any toast, rolls, muffins, crumpets etc on your menus. However, there are plenty of other foods that you can fill yourself up with as you may eat your fill of fat-free dairy products (natural or with aspartame), tuck into a soft-boiled egg and even a slice of lean chicken. You will feel as if you have enjoyed a very full breakfast – a little like having a full brunch every morning!

Moreover, this menu will be more energizing and balanced than a traditional breakfast of toast, muffins, crumpets etc or chocolatey cereals.

The oat bran galette

For some of my patients, mornings are the time of day when they most miss having the taste of bread. Others also complain about constipation. To get round these inconveniences and for die-hard bread fans, hearty eaters and people with constipation, I devised a galette recipe that can be included in the protein diet.

This came about when my daughter wanted to follow my diet. She used to feel ravenous all morning and had trouble keeping going until lunch. So she asked me what she could eat in the morning to 'fill' herself up more. I searched though my store cupboards and improvised an oat bran galette with some bran I had brought back from America and she thought it was excellent and nutritious. I honed the recipe and now oat bran is used systematically in my method. This galette is packed with soluble fibre and many recent studies have proved that by soaking up water, this soluble fibre forms a gel in the digestive tract. Nutrients get trapped in it and a few calories get taken away with this gel into the stools.

However, do remember that oat bran may only be eaten once a day. If you eat this galette several times a day, it will slow down the effects of the protein diet.

Make the most of your morning 'fat-burning' opportunity

When your body has not been fed, it digs into its fat cells to find some energy. This happens in the mornings when your stomach is empty. This process is called lipolysis and it often starts at night once your sugar reserves are used up. As soon as you get more energy by eating breakfast, it stops. Two ideas for making more of this natural 'fat-burning' phase are:

• Since your body will go straight for its fat reserves, if you are not too tired, take some exercise as soon as you wake up and before you have any breakfast.

• Follow the breakfast instructions for Phase 1 to the letter and have a hot drink and proteins. These will not halt the fat-burning process, so you will be able to benefit from it throughout the day.

Lunch

What can you eat for lunch in Phase 1?

You can devise your starters, main dishes and desserts based around the 72 protein foods listed on page 38. Eat as much as you want of them! You will also find on page 48 some menu ideas for a whole week. Make sure that you drink lots at mealtimes. You could make up a pot of green tea to go with your meal or have some sparkling water and so on. Soft drinks with artificial sweeteners are also allowed. Try using herbs and spices to add variety to what you eat and also take care with the presentation – nicely presented food is always more appetizing. To season your meat and eggs, refer back to pages 36 to 37. If you do not have time to prepare a sauce, you can easily add some vinegar, pepper, herbs or spices.

Be careful to avoid common errors that can slow down your diet and trigger water retention. Cut down on salt and mustard too.

DRINKS

Still or sparkling water

Green tea

Soft drinks with artificial sweeteners

STARTERS

Hard-boiled egg

Seafood sticks

Bresaola

Lean cooked meat (without any fat or rind)

Chicken breast

Tinned mackerel without the sauce

Smoked salmon

Prawns

Crab

MAIN COURSES

Grilled chicken

Steak tartare

Roast beef

Roast veal

Rabbit

Calf's liver

Steamed fish

Omelette

Scrambled eggs etc

DESSERTS

Virtually fat-free cottage cheese

Fat-free fromage frais

Fat-free quark

Fat-free yoghurt

Oat bran galette (if you did not eat one for breakfast)

Egg-based desserts

Sticking to your mealtime routine

It is important that you keep to a routine with your meals because otherwise after a few days you will end up feeling frustrated. Sitting down at the table to enjoy a hot meal is both convivial and comforting. Of course, for the time being your meals are made up of protein foods only, but you will discover that it is possible to devise tasty menus using just proteins.

With the menus you create, based on what you enjoy eating, try and make sure you have a separate starter, main course and dessert. Feel free to adjust your meals to match your appetite. For example, if you are stretched for time or never very hungry in the morning, then you can enjoy the oat bran galette as your lunchtime dessert.

Can I have a snack?

Of course you can allow yourself a snack as soon as you start to feel peckish, provided it is on the list of foods you are allowed.

Here are a few ideas for handy snacks that you can easily carry around with you:

- seafood sticks
- hard-boiled eggs
- fat-free yoghurt
- bresaola
- sliced ham, turkey or chicken (without any fat or rind)
- tea or coffee (without sugar or with sweetener)

Look after yourself

So that you allow your body time to digest your last meal, avoid eating too late and you will sleep better for it. Even if you are eating on your own, make yourself comfortable, get out a pretty tablecloth and set the table nicely for your spread – you should feel as if you are dining as normal. Make things cosy for yourself! Also, take your time over your meals. After you have been eating for 20 minutes, the feeling of hunger disappears. If you wolf your supper down, you will leave the table with your stomach still feeling empty.

Dinner

What can you eat for dinner in Phase 1?

More than any other meal (especially if you begin your diet in winter), your dinner must include a hot dish as this will fill you up and you will feel as if you have eaten a proper meal. You are allowed to eat the same foods as for lunch and you must structure your meal in the same way with a starter, main course and dessert. As a nice way to end your meal, you can make yourself a herbal tea or some chicory coffee, which will provide you with some of the water you need for your diet, as well as helping you to feel nice and replete.

DRINKS
Still or sparkling water
Herbal teas
Chicory coffee alternatives

STARTERS
Hard-boiled egg
Seafood sticks
Bresaola
Lean cooked meat (without any fat or rind)
Chicken breast
Tinned mackerel without the sauce
Smoked salmon
Prawns
Crab

MAIN COURSES
Grilled chicken
Steak tartare
Roast beef
Roast veal
Rabbit
Calf's liver
Steamed fish
Omelette
Scrambled eggs etc

DESSERTS
Virtually fat-free cottage cheese
Fat-free fromage frais
Fat-free quark
Fat-free yoghurt
Oat bran galette (if you did not eat one for breakfast)
Egg-based desserts

Don't give in!

Dinnertime is often a tricky time. Do you come home feeling tired? Do you have to cook the children's tea? Are you someone who fancies something to nibble on whilst getting dinner ready? Become aware of your own habits. If you know that dinnertime is the most difficult time of the day, then here is a tip to get through it: make yourself an oat bran galette and nibble on it while you cook. However, if you do this you cannot have a galette at any other time of the day.

No doubt you are going to have to sit down and eat with your family, deliberately avoiding eating foods you are not allowed whilst watching your children tuck into their pasta with relish. To resist temptation, go ahead and treat yourself to a snack before the meal. Avoid sitting down to eat feeling famished as this is bound to jeopardize your diet. Next, try and cook food for the rest of the family that you yourself are not especially keen on. Not that fond of rice? Then cook rice and you will find it easier not to give in and have some. Do not tempt fate – if you cannot resist bread and cheese, then don't give it to everyone else. Lastly, make absolutely sure that you include some parts of your diet in what everyone else eats, such as chicken or fish for the main course or fat-free fromage frais for dessert. Then you will feel as if you are eating with your family, even if you are not allowed some foods.

SOME SAMPLE MENUS FOR PHASE 1 (ATTACK)

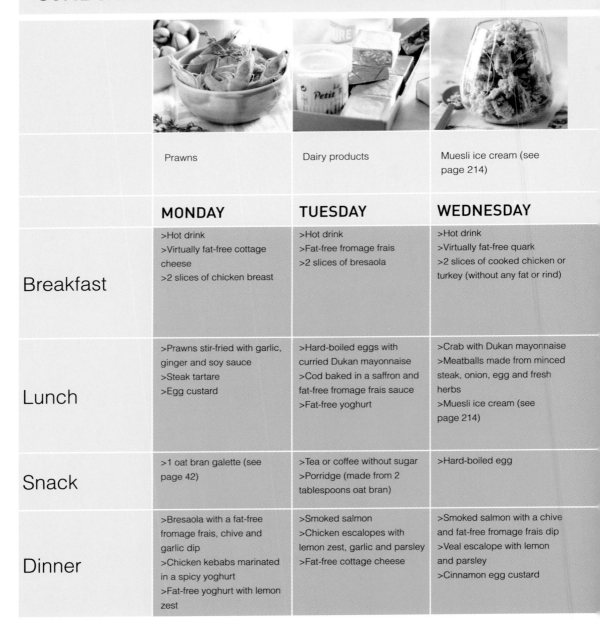

	Prawns	Dairy products	Muesli ice cream (see page 214)
	MONDAY	**TUESDAY**	**WEDNESDAY**
Breakfast	>Hot drink >Virtually fat-free cottage cheese >2 slices of chicken breast	>Hot drink >Fat-free fromage frais >2 slices of bresaola	>Hot drink >Virtually fat-free quark >2 slices of cooked chicken or turkey (without any fat or rind)
Lunch	>Prawns stir-fried with garlic, ginger and soy sauce >Steak tartare >Egg custard	>Hard-boiled eggs with curried Dukan mayonnaise >Cod baked in a saffron and fat-free fromage frais sauce >Fat-free yoghurt	>Crab with Dukan mayonnaise >Meatballs made from minced steak, onion, egg and fresh herbs >Muesli ice cream (see page 214)
Snack	>1 oat bran galette (see page 42)	>Tea or coffee without sugar >Porridge (made from 2 tablespoons oat bran)	>Hard-boiled egg
Dinner	>Bresaola with a fat-free fromage frais, chive and garlic dip >Chicken kebabs marinated in a spicy yoghurt >Fat-free yoghurt with lemon zest	>Smoked salmon >Chicken escalopes with lemon zest, garlic and parsley >Fat-free cottage cheese	>Smoked salmon with a chive and fat-free fromage frais dip >Veal escalope with lemon and parsley >Cinnamon egg custard

Don't forget your 2 tablespoons of oat bran, every day.

Scrambled eggs with salmon eggs (see page 134)

Bresaola

Oat bran galette (see page 42)

Spicy omelette with fresh mint (see page 172)

THURSDAY	FRIDAY	SATURDAY	SUNDAY
>Hot drink >Fat-free yoghurt >2 slices of cooked ham (without any fat or rind)	>Hot drink >Fat-free fromage frais >Porridge (made from 2 tablespoons oat bran)	>Hot drink >Virtually fat-free quark >1 oat bran galette (see page 42)	>Hot drink >Fat-free yoghurt >1 soft-boiled egg with chicken breast 'soldiers'
>Scrambled eggs with salmon roe (see page 134) >Grilled sea bass >Fat-free yoghurt	>Bresaola >Calamari with lemon juice, parsley and garlic >Fluffy pistachio mousses (see page 216)	>Tinned tuna mixed with fat-free fromage frais >Turkey escalope with a curried yoghurt sauce >Muesli ice-cream (see page 214)	>Scallops grilled in their shells with lime juice, coriander and chilli >Spicy egg white omelette with fresh mint (see page 172) >Fat-free cottage cheese
>2 slices of chicken breast	>2 fat-free yoghurts	>Bresaola	>Tea or coffee without sugar
>Mackerel without the sauce >Calf's liver pan-fried in a sherry or balsamic vinegar >Fat-free cottage cheese	>Seafood sticks >Rabbit with a mustard sauce (see page 182 and make without the chicory) >Fromage frais clementine creams (see page 226)	>Cooked chicken breast (without the skin) >Prawn and herb frittata >Fat-free yoghurt	>Smoked salmon purse filled with cottage cheese >Steak with a low-fat crème fraîche and mustard sauce >Egg custard

Fitting your diet
into your daily life
(Phase 1)

Eating with your family

You will be faced with many temptations, especially if you have children. So that you do not succumb, particularly in the Attack phase, you may well decide to feed the children separately and then get your own meal afterwards. To make it simpler, you could cook the proteins on their own (chicken in one dish, vegetables in another) so that you can select the food that suits you without disrupting your normal mealtime pattern. Make sure you increase the quantities of meat and keep serving yourself as much as you need so that you keep up with everyone else. This will also avoid your children asking questions as they might not understand why your plate is half empty. Prepare some 'mix-and-match' menus in advance that you can adapt. If, for example, your children love soft-boiled eggs, have an egg for yourself. You can use turkey strips as soldiers while your children eat bread.

Apéritif time

If you are having an apéritif at home, then you can prepare snacks that you can nibble away at without bending your diet rules, such as small prawns, seafood sticks and cubes of cooked turkey. Also, make sure that you have some sparkling water or Diet Coke so you can quench your thirst without being tempted by any alcohol or fruit juice. Replenish your glass yourself and never let it get completely empty. This way you will deter any polite guests, thinking they are being nice to you, from pouring you a little champagne or wine!

If you are invited out, the situation is not as easily managed, but it is not insurmountable. Before you go to your friends, start by filling yourself up with a suitable snack. Since vegetables are not allowed in the Attack phase, it is possible that you will not be able to eat any of the snacks on offer. If this is the case, ask for a big glass of sparkling water and hold it all the time as this will give you an excuse not to take any of the dishes the other guests are handing around.

At the restaurant

Here is a situation where the protein diet is easy to follow. You can start with an egg dish, some smoked salmon or even a seafood platter. You then have a wide choice for your main course: some grilled sirloin, a veal chop, fish or poultry. If the food takes some time to arrive, take care not to start nibbling food you are not allowed. If you feel that hunger might gnaw away at your stomach if you have to wait too long for your food, then eat something before you go out to the restaurant such as a boiled egg or seafood sticks.

For the cheese-lover or pudding fan, the difficulty comes after the main course when they risk being carried along by the other guests. Here the best defence strategy is to ask for a coffee and then you can order more if the conversation keeps going. Otherwise, keep a plain or fruit fat-free yoghurt in your car or office, then you can finish off your meal with the taste of a fresh, creamy dessert.

Eat lots and keep it varied!

Taste the foods listed and try them all out! During the first few days, you will tend to go for the foods you already know. But being on this diet is also an opportunity to be adventurous and discover new flavours. Visit your butcher and fishmonger and try out fish that frozen food manufacturers do not sell or certain meats you don't find in the supermarket.

Questions and answers

When I am on the diet should I take vitamins?

→ If the diet does not last long, taking vitamins is quite unnecessary. However, if the diet should stretch out over quite a long period, you can add a daily dose of multivitamin supplements, but avoid high doses and taking lots of different pills as they build up and can end up being toxic. You would do better to have a slice of calf's liver twice a week and 1 tablespoonful of brewer's yeast every morning. You can also make yourself mixed salads with plenty of lettuce, peppers, tomato, carrot and chicory as soon as vegetables are allowed.

Can I chew sugar-free chewing gum to take the edge off my hunger?

→ Chewing gum can prove very useful during a diet for snackers who are used to having something to chew in their mouth. To my mind, chewing gum is an excellent help in fighting weight problems. As you finish your last mouthful at dinner, go ahead and eat some chewing gum as it will stop you from 'raiding' your store cupboards.

Should I drink at mealtimes?

→ Failing to drink while you eat quite simply means that you run the risk of forgetting to drink. What is more, drinking while you eat increases the volume in your stomach, making you feel replete and satisfied. Lastly, water dilutes food, slows down its absorption and makes you feel full for longer. So yes, drink at mealtimes!

I have trouble drinking a lot, what can I do?

→ This quantity of liquid seems too much to you? Don't forget to include any tea, coffee or other infusion or herbal drink that you have. You will soon see that it is very easy to reach the minimum required. Also, remember to use water and the drinks you are allowed as a way of quelling hunger and making you feel fuller.

Can I do any sport in the Attack phase?

→ It all depends on how much weight you have to lose, your age and your medical history.

→ If you have a lot of weight to lose, it is preferable in the Attack, but also in the Cruise phase, not to expose the heart, circulation and hip, knee and vertebrae joints to any excessive effort.

→ If you are over 55, build up your exercise routine gradually, taking into consideration how overweight you are at the outset as well as the extra load this puts on your body.

→ On the other hand, if you are neither too old nor too heavy, anything is possible. However, during the Attack phase you are likely to lose weight at an astonishing speed and if combined with overexercising, this may tire you out and lessen the feeling of well-being that fuels your motivation both physically and mentally. Despite this, one form of exercise is almost always possible and that is walking. To my mind, walking is by far the best possible exercise and it's the simplest too. Natural and easy, you can go for a walk anywhere, at any time of the day, no matter what you weigh, without any special gear (you can even walk in heels) and without breaking into a sweat or injuring yourself. It costs nothing, but you'll reap a handsome reward.

Phase 1 summary

It's over – you have finished your Phase 1! Now it is time to take stock of how you feel and what you have lost.

You have lost a lot and very quickly

Since the Attack phase works at lightning speed, it is quite possible to lose 4 to 6 pounds in five days. However, someone who is obese will lose pounds more quickly at the start than a person who is already fairly slim and just wants to get their figure in trim for the summer holidays. Obese dieters can lose up to around 10 pounds.

You haven't lost weight as quickly as you had imagined

First of all, periods for most women are a time of high water retention. If this is true for you, drink a little less and use as little salt as possible. You will lose what you had expected a few days after the start of your period.

If this has nothing to do with periods, then take a closer look at your diet. Did you follow it absolutely to the letter?

The other possibility is that you are a more difficult case. Perhaps you have already tried lots of different diets, you have a strong genetic predisposition to putting on weight, you are experiencing the premenopause with a hormonal imbalance or you may even be taking antidepressants or cortisone?

You have been troubled by constipation

Proteins contain only very few waste products and not having fats reduces lubrication in the digestive tract. Drink a little more and go for water that is low in sodium.

You felt a little tired

Do you think the diet has made you feel tired? You were not tired before starting it?

If this is the case, this is quite uncommon, but it is possible. It may be down to you not eating enough. Don't forget that there is no restriction on quantity. Meat is the best natural fatigue-buster, especially red meat such as lean cuts of beef.

Tiredness connected with salt and water

Salt has an effect on blood pressure. If you don't have any salt in your food, you lower your blood pressure by 1 point and if it is low anyway – for example 11 – you could drop down to 10, or even 9, which is low and tiring.

Too much water (if you drink more than 2 litres) has the same effect. Water cleanses the blood and brings down blood pressure. When these are combined, it can cause the worst scenario. Try not to drink too much in the evenings. This will allow you to avoid getting up throughout the night as interrupted sleep will make you tired.

If the tiredness does not go away, get your doctor to check your blood pressure and let your doctor know that following a diet, as you are, does not usually make the dieter tired.

The Attack phase in a nutshell

You can eat 72 high protein foods and
nothing else.
This phase can last between one and ten
days. Focus on the foods you are allowed and
forget about all other food categories.

You can eat as much as you
want of these proteins.

You must drink at least 1.5 litres of water each day.
This is not a piece of advice, but an obligation.
For the diet to work, it is essential you drink copious amounts.

The eight food categories
you are allowed:
- lean meats, such as veal, rabbit
  and beef
- some offal
- all fish
- all shellfish
- poultry without the skin (but
  no duck or goose)
- lean sliced meats
- eggs
- fat-free dairy products

To season your food you can use:

- vinegar
- herbs
- spices
- drops of lemon juice
- a little salt
- mustard in moderation

To maximize pleasure, quantities are not restricted at all.
So that you feel good, do not limit quantities, but do vary your menus.

During the few Attack days, avoid all lapses.
This brief phase does not last long and is meant to take your body by surprise, so follow the instructions scrupulously.

You can have 1 or 2 tablespoonfuls of oat bran a day, especially in galettes.

Phase 2: **Cruise**

Go from 72 to 100 as-much-as-you want foods until you get down to the weight you want.

What you are aiming
for in Phase 2

Losing weight regularly

After five days in the Attack phase, you'll notice that the lack of vegetables and salad in your diet is starting to make itself felt. So you will have no trouble getting into this second phase, where you alternate days of pure proteins with days of proteins + vegetables.

Losing weight over the long haul

No doubt, you will notice that your weight loss slows down in this alternating phase. This is quite normal, as your body has to adjust itself to this new phase so that it can get into the diet over the long term. Don't worry, the weight loss from burning up fats is still continuing and although somewhat camouflaged by the return of water, it is nonetheless carrying on all the while.

As for how long this phase should last, this all depends on how many pounds you want to lose. It will last until you reach the weight you want to get down to.

Losing weight more steadily

If you have over 3 stone to lose, experience shows that on average you'll settle down to losing around a couple of pounds a week. Of course, during Phase 1 you lost a lot more, which is why within the space of a couple of months, in Phase 1 and Phase 2 combined, you can hope to lose your first stone and a half. We will then see this pattern gradually dip, since the body sets up a defence mechanism in the Consolidation phase. However, for the time being, if you follow the instructions to the letter, you should not encounter any obstacles.

The stepping-down-the-stairs effect

Whereas up until now your weight loss has been spectacular, all of a sudden your scales seem to be stuck. As soon as vegetables are introduced, water artificially flushed out by a protein-only diet comes back into your body, since the alternating phase is by definition less water-repellent than the pure protein phase. Of course, on pure protein days you'll be delighted to see your scales pointing in the right direction again. You'll feel as if your diet is advancing as if you were going down a staircase: stagnation as you rest on a step, then suddenly you drop down to the next step, and so on. Trust in the method, you will get down to your ideal weight without any problem.

The rules for
Phase 2

Introducing vegetables after the Attack period adds freshness and variety to the initial diet. It makes the diet easier and more comfortable. From now on, a good way to start your meals is with a well-seasoned salad, full of colour and flavour, or perhaps a soup on winter evenings. You can then move on to a main dish of meat or fish slowly cooked over flavourful, seasoned vegetables and, to finish it all off, have a dairy product, or two or three!

Alternating pure proteins and proteins + vegetables

During this second phase in your diet, you will alternate periods of pure proteins with periods of proteins + vegetables until you get down to the weight you want.

How you choose to alternate the two depends on your individual situation. Different parameters have to be taken into account, including age, digestion, how many pounds are to be lost, how much exercise you will do and how much you like meat and vegetables. Rhythms vary from one day pure proteins/one day proteins + vegetables to five days pure proteins/five days proteins +vegetables. We'll look at how you should choose the right one for you.

Whatever alternating rhythm you opt for, you can still eat as much as you want of both the proteins as well as the vegetables. This 'as-much-as-you-want' concept is one of the foundations of my method. The list of foods you are allowed does not change either (see page 38).

As much as you want, so you go the distance

Take care that you do not use this argument as some sort of token gesture. Faced with hunger, temptation, cravings and irresistible urges to snack, having this total freedom makes sense and it has a powerful role to play. However, it must not be some mere game or a way of keeping yourself busy.

I know some patients who settle down and chomp away without feeling hungry, as if they were chewing gum. Try and avoid this temptation. Vegetables are not that innocuous, so eat them only until

Vegetables yes, but on certain conditions

Provided you choose your vegetables from the list, you are allowed all these vegetables, raw or cooked, with no limit on quantity. You can eat them whenever you fancy. However, do take care to follow the instructions about how to prepare them so that you avoid increasing your fat intake, as you must cut out fats as far as possible.

you have completely satisfied your hunger. This does not change the principle at the heart of this diet – that quantities are not restricted – and however much you ingest you will continue losing weight, but at a less steady rate, which is of course less encouraging.

Pitfalls to avoid

• Worrying about your weight loss slowing down

Once vegetables are introduced, some patients who up until now have been following their instructions religiously, start to allow themselves an occasional small lapse. Often this is connected with the natural slowing down of the weight loss process, which had been extremely rapid in the Attack phase.

This slowing down is quite normal and would have come about anyway, even if you had carried on with the Attack phase. There are two reasons for this and they are related to each other. Firstly, surprised by the intensity of the attack, the body puts up little resistance to this powerful diet and it parts with its initial fat reserves easily. This surface fat is unstable and can be lost or regained very quickly. The protein diet is also very water-repellent, which means that as the initial fat gets burnt up water is suddenly expelled too. And 1 litre of water weighs a couple of pounds! After the first few days, these two factors that brought about your initial immediate loss, taper off. Finally, once vegetables appear, they are a third factor contributing to this slowing down. You are now involved in a quite different and fiercer battle and you will have to accept that this hand-to-hand combat will take longer.

• 'Nothing but vegetables'

As we are following a programme where one of the basic principles is your freedom to choose what you eat and how much, do not fall into the common trap of eating nothing but vegetables. Depriving yourself of proteins would be dangerous. What danger would you run? That of not getting the vital proteins you need, the proteins humans are unable to synthesize and that your body would take from your muscle mass, skin and hair. When vegetables are allowed, they must not replace meat and fish, but should be eaten alongside. Take a look at the list of vegetables on page 67. As with the Attack phase, take care to stick carefully to your instructions and work on the basis that if a food does not appear on the list, this means it is not allowed.

What should you do if you want to stop?

A diet is a little slice of life that can be affected by unpredictable factors as we encounter obstacles and difficulties.

• You may become weary of dieting and lose motivation. We are human and so tired and fragile at times.

• You may have to deal with pressure, stress, choices and difficulties. We are human and so get forced into things we do not choose.

• You may travel, go away or circumstances change from when you started and you have to stop dieting.

In all such situations, one rule must remain hard and fast inviolable. Yes, you may stop, but stick to the exit protocol. The very worst way out of your diet would be to beat a chaotic retreat. Such disarray would mean losing the results of your hard work. However much weight you have lost, you must keep it and protect it – it is yours. Go on to the third phase that you do not yet know about: the Consolidation phase (see page 85). This is a stage you have to go through between hard dieting and not dieting.

Alternating proteins
and vegetables

Why alternating is necessary

The Cruise diet, building on the momentum and speed generated by the pure protein Attack diet, is now responsible for guiding you to your chosen weight. This stage will therefore take up the largest part of the actual weight-loss section of the Dukan Diet.

The rhythmical addition of vegetables slows down the impact of the pure proteins. This is intended! You are not meant to keep up too rapid a rhythm as this would be counterproductive and it would force your body to put up fierce resistance. Wise housewives know that trying to squeeze a lemon in a single go does not work as well as having several goes and letting it rest in between. Protein days amount to an offensive, a surprise attack, and this attacking force has to consolidate its position and gather its strength so it can launch a fresh attack.

What is more, the body needs the freshness of vegetables and salads and their vitamins and fibre so that it can digest its food.

How do you choose how to alternate?

There are two main alternating rhythms and two less common ones for more unusual cases.

• Five days pure proteins (PP), then five days proteins + vegetables (PV)
This is a strong rhythm, often too strong, and it requires unswerving motivation. As time goes by, going for five days without any vegetables may seem too long.

• One day pure proteins (PP), then one day proteins + vegetables (PV)
In the past, I used to systematically recommend the five/five alternation, then I realized that the one/one rhythm often produced very similar results, but without the frustration of five days without vegetables, and it also caused less tension. So this is how I suggest you alternate.

• Two days pure proteins (PP), then five days proteins + vegetables (PV)
This way of alternating is less common and less intense and so is better suited to people who are vulnerable, fragile, older (over 70) and who, in particular, do not have much weight to lose. It is suitable too for anyone absolutely intent on losing weight slowly. Although few and far between, alternating like this suits such dieters well.

• Two days pure proteins (PP), followed by a normal diet for five days
A variation on the two/five rhythm is the two/zero, that is two days of pure proteins per week, then five normal days without any particular diet, but avoiding any excesses. This diet and pace best suit women with cellulite, who often have a very slim upper body, chest, bust and face, but ample hips and, in particular, very fleshy thighs. Especially when combined with a treatment, such as mesotherapy, for specific areas, this diet can produce the best results for targeted areas, while sparing the upper body as much as possible.

In this case, it is best to schedule any treatment sessions for those specific areas on a protein day so that any stubborn fat is tackled, freed from where it is trapped and burnt up.

Eat cold food and you'll lose weight quicker

Did you know that when you eat cold food your body has to heat it to bring it up to body temperature so that it can be digested and, most importantly, assimilated? Nothing goes into your blood without being heated beforehand. Heating up food uses up calories and these calories are taken from the ones supplied by your food intake – it all adds up!

Eating cold food is not always easy, especially in wintertime. However, you can have cold drinks. Whenever you drink 1.5 litres of water from the fridge, its temperature is 4°C/39.2°F. When you pass this water in your urine, it is now 35°C/95°F, so you have raised the temperature of this water by 31°C/87.8°F. You have heated it up and burnt calories. Not many of course, but they mount up by the end of the year. So, if you enjoy cold water carry on drinking it, and if not, have another go.

What can you eat
in Phase 2?

During this Cruise phase, you are allowed 100 foods, without any restriction on quantity, time of day or combination.

For pure protein days (PP), refer back to the list of foods allowed in Phase 1 on page 38.

However, for proteins + vegetables days (PV), here is the list of vegetables you can go ahead and enjoy, cooked or uncooked. Don't forget to combine them with proteins.

Allowed		Tolerated	Not allowed
Artichoke	Leek	Beetroot	Avocado
Asparagus	Mushroom	Carrot	Broad beans
Aubergine	Onion		Dried beans and peas
Broccoli/Purple sprouting	Palm heart	**Tolerated**	Lentils
broccoli	Pepper	**Condiments**	Peas
Cabbage (all types,	Pumpkin/Marrow/Squash		Potatoes
including natural	Radish	Cornflour	Salsify
sauerkraut)	Rhubarb	Fat-reduced cocoa	Sweetcorn
Celery/Celeriac	Salad leaves	powder	
Chicory	Soya beans	Emmenthal (5% fat)	
Courgette	Spinach	Low-fat crème fraîche	
Cucumber	Swede	(3% fat)	
Fennel	Swiss chard	Sesame seeds/poppy	
French beans/String	Tomato	seeds	
beans/Mangetout	Turnip	White wine (for cooking)	

How should you
prepare vegetables?

Raw

For anyone who can digest raw vegetables, it is always preferable to eat vegetables when they are completely fresh and uncooked so that you avoid losing any of their vitamins.

Despite appearing harmless, dressings pose one of the major problems for weight-loss. Indeed, for many people the quintessential diet food is crudités and salads, low in calories and high in fibre and vitamins. This is absolutely correct, but fails to take into account the dressing that comes with them, which puts paid to all these wonderful qualities.

For these reasons, throughout the whole weight-loss phase you must only use the dressings listed below:

• **Dukan vinaigrette**
1 tablespoon Dijon mustard or Meaux à l'ancienne
5 tablespoons balsamic vinegar
1 teaspoon vegetable oil
1 garlic clove
7-8 basil leaves, chopped
Salt and black pepper

Take an old mustard jar and fill it with all the ingredients, mixing very thoroughly. If you like garlic, leave a clove to marinate in the bottom of the jar.

• **Dukan mayonnaise**
1 egg yolk
1 tablespoon Dijon mustard
3 tablespoons virtually fat-free fromage frais or quark
1 tablespoon chopped parsley or chives
Salt and black pepper

Watch out for oil

In an ordinary salad bowl containing 2 large lettuces and 2 tablespoonfuls oil, the salad accounts for 20 calories and the oil for 280 calories. Be on the lookout for oil, it is not one of the foods you are allowed. Olive oil is no exception to this rule. The benefits of this oil are universally recognized and it plays an important role in protecting us from cardiovascular disease, nevertheless it still contains just as many calories as any other oil on the market.

Put the egg yolk in a mixing bowl and combine with the mustard. Season with salt and pepper and add the herbs. Gradually mix in the fromage frais or quark, stirring continuously. Mayonnaise must be kept chilled.

• Yoghurt or fromage frais dressing

You can make up a natural, tasty dressing using a non-fat dairy product.

You can even use some ordinary natural yoghurt. It is hardly any more calorific than non-fat yoghurt, but it is creamier. Add one level tablespoonful of mustard (Dijon if possible) and beat the mixture so it thickens like mayonnaise and has a nice consistency. Then add a dash of vinegar, salt, black pepper and herbs.

Ways of cooking vegetables

• Steaming

The vegetables you are allowed may be cooked in water or, even better, steamed to retain the maximum amount of vitamins.

• In the oven

You may also bake them in the oven in the juices from your meat or fish. Examples of typical dishes are sea bass with fennel, sea bream with tomatoes and cabbage stuffed with minced beef.

• En papillote (in aluminium foil)

Cooking vegetables in aluminium foil combines all the advantages of taste and nutritional value. This is a particularly good way of cooking fish. Salmon, for example, remains moist when cooked on a bed of leeks or chopped aubergines.

• 'Plancha' grilling

Either use a real plancha (flat stove-top) grill pan or a heavy-based non-stick frying pan or ridged chargrill pan. This is a fantastic way to cook vegetables as it gives them a different taste and texture. I would particularly recommend it to anyone not overly fond of vegetables. Try it with your children if they turn their noses up at these essential foods.

Don't forget your spices!

Recent studies have shown just how important are taste sensations and the quantity and variety of flavours in making us feel satisfied and satiated.

Nowadays, we know that certain spices provide intense flavours, especially cloves, ginger, star anise and cardamom. They bring together strong, penetrating sensations that work on the hypothalamus, the area in our brain that measures these sensations, until it reaches such a point that the feeling of satiety is triggered. So it is very important to use the whole range of these spices as much as possible, preferably at the start of a meal. If you are not already a diehard fan, do try and get used to them.

Prescribed
physical exercise

Up until recently, I used to strongly recommend exercise, but I did not include it categorically as an integral part of my programme. Nowadays, I do not think twice before writing it out on a prescription for my patients. PE (prescribed exercise) is the second driving force behind my method.

Walking as weight-loss medicine

So, for the past couple of years I have stopped just advising my patients to walk, I now prescribe it like a medicine.

Attack phase	20 minutes/per day
Cruise phase	30 minutes/per day
Consolidation phase	30 minutes/per day
Stabilization phase	20 minutes/per day
To 'break through a stagnation plateau'	1 hour/per day for three days

When you consider all the effort, expenditure, restrictions and motivation you need to lose weight, what is a 20-minute walk in the big scheme of things? So, I am counting on you.

Walking is the activity that:

• is most natural for humans. If we are no longer apes, this is because we stood up and walked;
• is by far the most effective. Walking at a brisk pace burns off more energy than playing tennis, as on court you only play physically for 20 out of 60 minutes;
• is the least costly;
• can be undertaken at any time of the day or night;
• least injures or damages our joints;
• makes us sweat the least;
• allows us to do other things at the same time e.g. make phone calls, listen to music, even read a book;

- makes us least hungry;
- can even be undertaken by the obese without any risk;
- you are most likely to stick with for a long time once you have felt and understood its extraordinary benefits.

There are, of course, many other ways of being active – going to the gym, exercise bikes, fitness coaches, martial arts, swimming, dancing and tennis etc. However, all these forms of exercise, however useful they may be, are add-ons to being physically active. Although useful, they cannot lay claim to what walking alone is entitled to assert: its universal status as being what all human bodies are built to do. And as such, it offers the best way of giving your diet a powerful boost.

By walking, you are doing nothing less than adding a second general to your army to help fight your weight problems!

Purposeful activity as part of your daily life

Purposeful activity involves doing everything you would have had to do before developments in technology freed you from doing them. If you have a weight problem, you need to try and change your attitude towards physical effort. You are not leading the life for which you were naturally intended and this is making you put on weight. Nowadays, our bodies suffer because they no longer carry out the minimum physical activity required to maintain their muscle function. Not making enough use of our bodies prevents us from burning up surplus calories from our food and leaves us with restriction and dieting as the only ways of avoiding or limiting weight gain. But more seriously, no longer being physically active – what we deem to be progress – deprives us of a part of ourselves, what the Greeks termed our 'physical humanity'. Our psyche, our feelings and emotions, our physiological equilibrium and our hormonal and immune systems all feel the effects of this. What we are missing out on will express itself in subconscious suffering that sooner or later will seek comfort in food.

Apart from walking, which is the basis of our natural physical activity, I favour purposeful activity in our daily lives. This is activity that you must try, in part, to wrest back from the machines and gadgets that stop you from being active.

What started me thinking about PE

Two events set the idea in motion:

The first was when queuing in a Spanish travel agency I noticed that the three members of staff were seated on chairs with casters. Two of them used the chairs to propel themselves 2 or 3 metres to fetch files or print off tickets, but the third employee always got up and, by coincidence, he was slim whereas the other two were far from it.

The second was when I was treating a patient who has since become my friend. When I first met him, he weighed over 36 stone. Once he got down to just over 22 stone, he decided to give up smoking and stopped losing weight. I was all for helping him stabilize his weight, but he was desperately keen to lose a bit more. So I wrote him out a prescription for a daily 45-minute walk that he absolutely had to stick to. He did it, despite being reluctant and a very senior managing director. Today he weighs just under 16 stone.

• Forget about lifts and escalators

A woman aged 30 to 40 who complains about having to walk up four flights of stairs to my surgery because the lift is not working is a woman who has 'lost her body'.

Going up and down five steps uses up 1 calorie. Four flights, twice a day over a year, adds up to 1,400 calories, which means your scales will register a loss of over 4 pounds of fat.

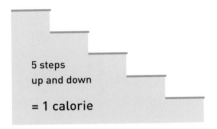

5 steps
up and down

= 1 calorie

• Don't forget ordinary household tasks

>Do the hoovering without sparing any effort. Work the hoover as you would work the machines you pay for in a gym.

>Walk to the shops to do your shopping and take pride in doing this.

>Walk your dog.

>Make your bed, but make it properly. Do not bend your back and put pressure on your spine, bend your knees instead.

>Do not shy away from carrying any sort of object or packet.

>Whenever you pick something up off the ground, always bend your knees and never your back!

>Do the gardening! This is a great way of burning up calories.

My Dukan special exercise

This exercise works the thighs, shoulders and dorsal (back) muscles and you do it in bed once before you go to sleep and once before you get up.

• At the top of your bed, position a pillow against the wall and lean a cushion on the pillow to make a 45° inclined plane.

• Move yourself into a seated position so that your chest follows the same angle/incline as your cushion. Bend your knees to almost 90°.

• Raise yourself from your inclined position into a vertical position and go down again until you touch the back of the cushion. Do this exercise between 10 and 30 times in succession.

• As soon as you feel your stomach muscles getting tired, alter the exercise. Raise your chest up by pulling up only with your arms. The benefit of this is that you can let your stomach rest while your arms work and you can continue this simple, quick exercise without getting tired. And once your biceps start to warm up, you can use your stomach muscles again.

• Start off by doing this 15 times in the morning and 15 times at night. The goal, which is easily achievable, is to manage to do this, within a few days or weeks, 200 times in the morning and 200 times at night, in a session that lasts no more than a few minutes.

What is so 'special' about this exercise?

It exercises the muscles around your stomach that naturally, in both men and women, go slack with age. It tenses your arm muscles, where you see the first signs of any slackening in the skin. It also works the thighs, shoulders and back muscles. And you can do it in bed.

So if you were to do just one exercise, it should be this one.

Roll on wintertime!

By walking at a temperature around 0°C, you use up an extra 25% calories. Go out wearing enough, but not too much. Wrap up just enough so you don't feel cold and you avoid catching a cold.

SOME SAMPLE MENUS FOR PHASE 2 (CRUISE)

	Smoked salmon purse filled with mussels (see page 142)	Salmon and cucumber millefeuilles (see page 144)	Tofu choc cream (see page 220)
	MONDAY	**TUESDAY**	**WEDNESDAY**
Breakfast	>Hot drink >Fat-free fromage frais >Oat bran porridge made with hot milk and sweetener	>Hot drink >Scrambled eggs with herby mushrooms >Bresaola	>Hot drink >Fat-free natural yoghurt >1 oat bran galette (see page 42) with an egg and smoked salmon
Lunch	>Smoked salmon purse filled with mussels (see page 142) >Chicken escalope with a fried egg, parsley and cornichons >Fluffy pistachio mousse (see page 216)	>Salmon and cucumber millefeuilles (see page 144) >Mediterranean cockles (see page 180) >Rhubarb compote (see page 230)	>Mediterranean prawns in a vanilla sauce (see page 138) >Medallions of sole and salmon (see page 174) >Iced crème anglaise (see page 238 and serve without the pineapple)
Snack	>Home-made custard	>1 oat bran galette (see page 42)	>Seafood sticks
Dinner	>Prawns with dill Dukan mayonnaise >Tofu and ham quiche (see page 190 and replace the mushrooms and cherry tomatoes with ham) >Fat-free flavoured yoghurt	>Crevettes and cherry tomatoes in a spicy cream (see page 146) >Aniseed-flavoured veal stew with fennel (see page 186) >Fat-free natural yoghurt	>Moules marinière >Chicken breast with herbes de Provence >Tofu choc cream (see page 220)
	→ PP	→ PV	→ PP

Here you are alternating one PP (pure proteins) day with one PV (proteins + vegetables) day + 2 tablespoons of oat bran, every day.

| Baked vegetable terrine (see page 149) | Iced chocolate soufflés (see page 216) | Stir-fried beef with sweet peppers (see page 200) | Pan-fried scallops with a vanilla foam (see page 140) |

THURSDAY	FRIDAY	SATURDAY	SUNDAY
>Hot drink >1 oat bran galette (see page 42) with grilled tomatoes and herbs >Non-fat cottage cheese	>Hot drink >Omelette >Lean turkey slices	>Hot drink >Non-fat cottage cheese >1 oat bran galette (see page 42) made with coriander and chilli, roasted tomatoes and fat-reduced bacon	>Hot drink >Virtually fat-free quark >Lean ham slices
>Baked vegetable tagine (see page 149) >Rabbit with mustard sauce and braised chicory (see page 182) >Fat-free yoghurt	>Mini smoked salmon vol-au-vents (see page 132) >Chicken breast wrapped in bresaola, sprinkled with herbs and baked in foil >Iced chocolate soufflé (see page 218)	>Cucumber appetizers with red roe (see page 152) >Stir-fried beef with sweet peppers (see page 200) >St. Tropez tart (see page 222)	>Pan-fried scallops with a vanilla foam (see page 140) >Veal escalope with a herb and mustard crust >Muesli ice cream (see page 214)
>Edamame beans sprinkled with chilli powder and sea salt	>1 oat bran galette (page 42) and cinnamon	>Lean ham slices	>Fat-free yoghurt
>Salmon and broccoli mousse (see page 150) >Asian-style mussels (see page 184) >Fromage frais creams (see page 226 and make without the clementines)	>Oysters with a shallot and red wine vinegar dipping sauce >Fillet of sole with tarragon and lemon >Gingerbread with a spoon of crème fraîche (3% fat) (see page 224)	>Strips of chargrilled courgette and red pepper tossed in a Dukan vinaigrette >Carrot flan (see page 188) with grilled chicken >Lemony mousse (see page 236)	>Seafood sticks >Roast chicken with lemon and tarragon gravy >Grand Marnier Swiss roll (see page 228)
→ PV	→ PP	→ PV	→ PP

Fitting your diet into
your daily life (Phase 2)

When you are with others, the Cruise phase is simpler to manage since you can eat more foods, but at the same time it is also more complex as the temptations are greater and it is easier to lose control.

Eating with your family

If you have children, prepare their starchy foods, such as pasta, rice or potatoes, separately. Steam the vegetables and put some to one side for yourself. You can always pan-fry the rest of the vegetables for those who want to be more indulgent. For anyone who does not have much time, here is a very simple tip to avoid preparing lots of different dishes. Place the steamed vegetables on the table for everyone, along with some extra-virgin olive oil (full of omegas), which the others can use for seasoning. Children just love broccoli if you sprinkle over hazelnut oil or sugar snap peas drizzled with walnut oil. As for you, you have to eat your vegetables without any oil, so make sure you have all your favourite spices out on the table so you can season them to your taste.

Apéritif time

If you are entertaining guests at home, you now have a wider choice than in Phase 1. Fill up dishes with vegetable crudités and cherry tomatoes, then you can nibble away without any qualms. You have a wide choice, including seafood sticks, strips of ham and vegetables. Once again, the danger may lurk in the dressing, especially when you are invited out. The vegetables already have dressing on them? Then leave them well alone. Of course, if there are any dips in separate dishes, you must avoid dipping your vegetables in them. Lastly, if you are invited to a friend who loves serving vol-au-vents and little pastries as appetizers, then remember to fill yourself up beforehand with a boiled egg or a few seafood sticks and go for the 'glass in hand' tactic: fill up a glass with sparkling water and make sure you keep filling it up so you are not served an unwanted glass of champagne! Having your hands full will also keep other guests from passing you the nibbles.

At the restaurant

From the menu you can choose meat, fish and vegetables. Always check with the waiter how the vegetables are cooked. If they have any sauce or dressing, order a green salad instead without any dressing. If you plan ahead, you can take along some Dukan vinaigrette in your bag to season your meal yourself. Otherwise, try mixing your pieces of meat in with your salad so it does not seem too bland.

Place the bread basket (not allowed) out of your reach. If you like mustard, you can put a little on the side of your plate. Its acidity may help if you have to wait a long time to be served, by taking the edge off your appetite.

Questions and answers

In the Cruise phase, are you allowed fat-free yoghurts with fruit?

→ There is no restriction on fat-free natural yoghurt and non-fat 'flavoured' yoghurts are also allowed, 'as much as you want'. As for non-fat yoghurt containing fruit bits or purée, the answer is, 'possibly, but the maximum is two fruit yoghurts per day'. This can be tolerated if your weight is dropping as expected. If you are shedding it slowly, then do not have more than one of these yoghurts per day. If your weight is stagnating, stop eating them altogether.

Is it possible to eat carrots and beetroot every day?

→ Carrots and beetroot are known for being sweet and indeed they are. Although they do not contain as much sugar as people think, these are sugars that get rapidly absorbed, particularly when cooked.

→ If you are tempted to overindulge and eat them too frequently, then avoid these two vegetables.

In the Cruise phase, are you allowed mustard and, if so, how much?

→ Normal or Dijon mustard, yes, without any restriction. Grain mustard also works well, mixed with balsamic vinaigrette.

→ On the other hand, avoid mustards, like honey ones, that have too much sugar. If you tend to suffer from water retention, also go easy on mustard as it contains salt.

I have reintroduced vegetables and my weight loss has slowed down, am I going to put weight back on?

→ It is quite normal for your weight loss to slow down, but don't worry, you are not going to put any weight back on. In Phase 1, eating pure proteins enabled you to quickly lose fat and water. This diet is water-repellent and the proteins flush out water. When you add vegetables, you are also adding water and mineral salts, so the diet becomes much less water-repellent. You will continue to lose weight, but more slowly, as a little of the water you flushed out is being replaced, which tends to camouflage the fat that is lost. When you weigh yourself, it looks as if your weight is stagnating.

→ However, alternating in the Cruise phase allows the diet to continue being very effective. As soon as you eat pure proteins again, you will see another drop in your weight. If your scales do seem to be stuck, it is really important not to get downhearted as eating anything you are not allowed can upset the system and provide it with valid reasons to stagnate.

Phase 2 summary

You lose weight going from plateau to plateau

During Phase 2, your body will go into cruise speed. You will not lose weight as quickly as in Phase 1 but, going from plateau to plateau, you will lose the pounds you want to. During the first two months, you will gradually lose your first 18 to 22 pounds (1 stone 4 lbs to 1 stone 8lbs). The plateaus that you will notice are to do with vegetables being included again and the amount of water they provide. Whatever you do, you must not lose heart when your weight loss slows down as this is to be expected. If you are experiencing the menopause, at the end of your menstrual cycle or if you have already tried many diets before this one, your body may also be more stubborn. Do not give in – your body is the one that will eventually give way. The best way of forcing your way through is to walk (1 hour per day for three days).

And should you feel your motivation weaken

After the euphoria of Phase 1, when you lost pounds like never before, you are going to find that Phase 2 is much slower. The danger comes from having this impression. So you will need to tell yourself, and keep on saying to yourself, that by following these instructions to the letter you will manage to lose weight, keep it off and keep it stable over the long term.

And time is not your foe. Remember that once your target weight is attained, your goal is to learn how to maintain it over time.

So that you successfully complete this stage, concentrate on your instructions rather than on your scales. Copy out the list of vegetables you are allowed, do your shopping in advance so that you never run out of anything and make up suitable sauces and dressings so that no crafty calories start sneaking their way back into your menus. Be objective and note down carefully what you have eaten in the day; your vigilance will pay off. Tell yourself that the longer the list of foods you are allowed, the greater the temptations, so you run a greater risk of your diet ending in failure. You need therefore to be even more vigilant than you were in Phase 1.

You have had some lapses

What's the big deal? You have lost a day, you add a half hour walk to your daily routine or you go onto pure proteins the next day and everything will go back to normal again. Don't dwell on it and, most importantly, don't feel guilty.

You have given up... all is not lost

Take a deep breath and, with me at your side, get back on track. There is no question of you being left by the wayside. If you have given up, then there must have been a good reason for it. Generally, it is some difficulty or major stress, feeling depressed or losing motivation. All that matters is that you avoid beating a retreat in a chaotic manner, forfeiting all you have achieved and losing the results of your hard work. These results are yours and you should protect them. To do this, if you really have to stop, then take the proper exit route and go straight into Consolidation, Phase 3, sticking to the rule that it lasts five days for every pound lost. Then go into Stabilization. And as soon as you feel your motivation return, you will feel proud of yourself for not falling apart at the seams and be ready to have another go, and keep on going, until you reach your set target.

The Cruise phase in a nutshell

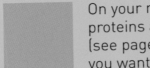

On your menu, you can keep the proteins allowed from the Phase 1 list (see page 38), still eating as much as you want.

And now you can add to your menu all the vegetables.

How about tomatoes, cucumber, radishes, spinach, asparagus, leeks, French beans, cabbage, mushrooms, celery, fennel, salad leaves, Swiss chard, aubergine, courgettes, peppers and even carrots and beetroot, as long as you don't eat these at every meal.

As with the proteins, you can eat as much as you want of the vegetables.

Take care with salad dressings, more than a teaspoon of oil is not allowed.

You must walk 30 minutes per day and do your Dukan special exercise. If your weight stagnates, increase this to a 60-minute walk for three days.

Alternating

In the Cruise phase, alternate between periods of proteins and vegetables and periods of proteins without vegetables until you reach your target weight.

Choose your alternating rhythm and stick to it.

One day pure proteins, one day proteins+vegetables or five days/five days. If you don't have too much weight to lose, you can opt for two days/five days or two days pure proteins and five days on a normal diet.

You will carry on eating

1 to 2 tablespoonfuls of oat bran per day.

Phase 3:
Consolidation

Once you have reached your True Weight, you go into the
Consolidation phase, a transition phase between dieting and
not dieting that you must pass through.

What you are aiming
for in Phase 3

For every pound lost, spend five days in Consolidation

You are going to consolidate the weight you have got down to by spending 5 days in the Consolidation phase for every pound lost. In other words, if you have lost 10 pounds, you have to follow this phase for 50 days, if you have shed 60, you will have to stick with it for 300 days. But don't worry, even if Consolidation is a tricky period, you can eat foods again that up until now have not been allowed. Your menus will therefore be more varied and there will be plenty for you to enjoy.

An 'attainable and maintainable' target weight

To work out your True Weight, you need advice from a specialist based on all the parameters that play a part in choosing how to determine this crucial weight.

To work it out, you must include the maximum weight you have ever reached, which leaves its traces; your minimum weight; the weight you have been at for the longest time in your life; as well as the weight you dream of attaining. Gender and age must also be taken into account. After the age of eighteen, your True Weight goes up every decade by just over 2 pounds for a woman and 2½ pounds for a man. Depending on whether your bone structure is fine or heavy, means you can also add or subtract a couple of pounds. Finally, you need to account for the number of diets you have already tried and whether there is a family history of weight problems. Everyone's weight problems are unique. To calculate precisely and decide your True Weight, go to my website www.dukandiet.co.uk, fill in the questionnaire and you will have your True Weight straightaway.

A crucial transition phase

During your first two phases, Attack then Cruise, you lost weight and your body fought to hold on to its reserves, but it lost the battle.

Whilst this struggle was going on, it developed a dual reaction that you should know about: profit + economy.

• **Increased profit:** the more weight you lose, the greater the energy your body extracts from every last morsel of food. At the stage you are at now, this is getting on for 100%.

• **Greater economy:** the more weight you lose, the more your body strives to cut down on energy used for metabolic, hormonal and digestive functions.

Consequently, it is vital you do not feed this greedy and miserly body with overly rich foods from which it will try and extract every last calorie.

Fighting the rebound effect

Fortunately for you, with time your body will ease off and stop reacting in such an extreme way if it senses that you are starting to feed it again with a more open, varied and energizing diet. During this period, you are vulnerable. Drawing on my experience, I managed to work out how long this vulnerability lasts – it is proportional to the weight lost.

How long Consolidation lasts: five days for every pound lost. Yes! It is that simple. If you have lost 10 pounds, then your Consolidation will have to last 50 days and for 20 pounds lost = 100 days.

Why is there a rebound effect?

Your body reacts to its reserves being plundered by gradually reducing the energy it uses and, in particular, by stepping up as far as possible the amount it can extract and assimilate from anything you eat. You are therefore sitting on top of a volcano and in possession of a body that is eagerly awaiting just the right moment to replenish its lost reserves. A copious meal that would have had little impact before the start of the diet, now, at the end of the diet, will have far-reaching repercussions.

How long does a rebound effect last?

The rebound effect carries on throughout the whole Consolidation phase, that is five days for every pound lost. Instructions about the length of the Consolidation phase that are too vague, and the euphoria felt after victoriously shedding those unwanted pounds, often jeopardize the diet if this instruction about length of time is not adhered to precisely.

The rules for
Phase 3

The whole time you are consolidating the weight you have slimmed down to, you will follow as closely as possible the following diet.

Length: five days for every pound lost

Keep in mind that half of all diets fail in the first three months after dieters achieve the weight they wanted to be at.

Also, take note that this Consolidation phase offers you a balanced diet, but in no way is it a diet that is meant to make you lose weight. Following the instructions for Phase 3 means you are guaranteed to consolidate the weight you have achieved. You must not miss out any of the rules, and especially not the rule about time: five days for every pound lost, which is about the time your body needs to forget about and come to terms with the weight it used to be. During this period, you are going to slowly retrain your body and appetite and give it back a little freedom, but only a little: you are still on probation!

Reintroducing foods that were not allowed, but in very precise quantities

As well as the protein foods and vegetables from Phase 2, you will at last be allowed bread, fruit, cheese and some starchy foods. Eating certain dishes and pleasurable foods will also be possible. However, take note, you must adhere to the strict order in which they are introduced and to a set of instructions that are specific enough to prevent you from losing control in any way.

• 1 serving of fruit per day

In practice, this means all fruit, except grapes, bananas, cherries and dried fruit. Fruit is a healthy food, packed with vitamins, but it is rich, essentially in sugars that tend to be rapid-assimilation sugars. So the fruit you eat has to be supervised and, for the time being, you must keep to one serving per day. Eating fruit is not harmless and we often forget that it also naturally contains sugars that we directly assimilate. Think of one serving = one unit, that is one apple, one pear, one orange, one grapefruit, one peach or one nectarine. As for small fruit, use a small dish so one unit = one dish of strawberries or raspberries. For larger fruit, such as melon or watermelon, cut them in half. For medium-sized fruit, have up to two, such as two apricots or two plums etc.

• 2 slices of wholemeal bread per day
You can eat them at any time of the day: for breakfast, as a lunchtime sandwich with cold meat or ham, or even in the evening with a portion of cheese.

• 40g (1½oz) mature cheese per day
You are allowed to eat all hard-rind cheeses, such as Cheddar ,Gouda or Tomme dr Savoie (difficult to find but worth it as it is a marvellous cheese). For now, avoid soft-rind cheeses, such as Camembert, blue cheeses and goat's cheeses. One serving equals 40g (1½ oz).

Please note: make sure you eat this portion in a single go so you avoid making mistakes with quantities and nibbling at any extra cheese.

• 2 servings of starchy foods per week
Avoid white rice and potatoes.

>Pasta
The starchy food best suited for our particular use is pasta, as it is made from hard wheat whose vegetable texture is very resistant. This resistance slows down digestion. Nowadays, you can also buy wholemeal pasta. Moreover, everyone likes pasta and it is rarely associated with the idea of 'dieting'. It is easy to introduce pasta into your menus. However, be careful what you have with it: butter, oil, cream and cheese will double the calories in your bowl of pasta. Give yourself a proper serving (220g/8oz cooked pasta) and choose a light accompanying sauce made from fresh tomatoes, onions and spices.

>Couscous, polenta and bulgar wheat
You are allowed 220g (8oz) servings.

Cooking your couscous without adding fat

Place the couscous in a terracotta dish, mix a stock cube with some water to give it flavour and pour this over the couscous, covering it and leaving at least one centimetre of water above. Let the couscous soak this up and swell for 20 seconds, then put it in a microwave oven for 1 minute. Remove the dish from the microwave, fluff it up with a fork to get rid of any lumps. Put it back in the microwave for another minute, then it is ready!

Eat slowly and think about what you are eating

Pleasurable foods are included again in this phase of the diet. Enjoy them! Eating them slowly will lessen your appetite since, after 20 minutes, you will start to feel satiated. You can also learn to savour all these textures and flavours that up until now have not been allowed. Get into the habit of taking your time, particularly if before dieting you were used to wolfing down your food.

>Brown rice

This is as good to eat as white rice and the measure is 220g (8oz). However, wait a while longer before eating white rice and potatoes as they contain sugars that, for the time being, get assimilated a little too 'rapidly'.

>Lentils

With some of the 'slowest' sugars that exist, lentils are very filling and have an extremely high iron content. You are allowed one 220g (8oz) serving, but do not add any fat. Kidney beans, dried peas and split peas are also allowed in the same rations and without any fat.

• **1 portion of leg of lamb or roast pork fillet per week**

Avoid the outer slice of your leg of lamb at all costs, as it is too fatty and if overcooked this surface fat can be carcinogenic. As for roast pork, make sure it is fillet and steer clear of any cuts from along the spine as they are far too fatty. You are free to eat cooked ham, but as yet you are still not allowed cured hams, such as Parma ham.

Two celebration meals per week

Twice a week, you will be able to enjoy a meal when you can eat whatever you like without worrying about whether the foods are allowed or not. Please note that this means two meals a week and not two days a week. My patients often mix this up. One celebration meal means one starter of your choice, one main course, one dessert and one glass of wine. But be careful! You may eat all this, provided you abide by one specific condition: that you never take second helpings of the same dish and you eat and drink one 'unit' of everything. Furthermore, celebration meals are never eaten in succession. Leave at least one day between the two meals to allow your body time to clear out any surplus.

One day of pure proteins per week

This day of pure proteins will guarantee that you do not put any weight back on. So you will only be allowed to eat the Attack phase proteins (see the list on page 38), with no limit on quantity. Just a little more effort, it is the only restriction there is in this Consolidation phase. As far as you possibly can, keep Thursdays as a pure protein day.

What can you eat
in Phase 3?

At last, the range of foods you are allowed opens up! You are going to enjoy being able to eat certain foods once more that you have not eaten in a long time.

You are of course allowed the Phase 1 proteins (see the list on page 38) as well as all the vegetables reintroduced in Phase 2 (see the list on page 67). In addition, you may eat the following foods, while sticking to the frequency and quantities laid down in the rules. You may eat foods that are 'not allowed' at your celebration meals.

Fruit (1 portion per day)

Allowed	Not allowed
Apple	Almonds
Apricot	Banana
Blackberry	Cashew nuts
Clementine	Cherries
Grapefruit	Grapes
Melon	Hazelnuts
Nectarine	Peanuts
Orange	Pistachios
Peach	Walnuts
Pear	
Plum	
Raspberry	
Strawberry	
Watermelon etc.	

Bread (2 slices per day)

Allowed	Not allowed
Wholemeal bread	Baguette
Wholewheat bread	Sandwich bread
	White bread

Cheese (1 serving per day)

Allowed	**Not allowed**
Cheddar	Blue cheese
Edam	Brie
Emmental	Camembert
Gouda	Goat's cheese
Gruyère	(soft rind)
Leicester	
Manchego	
Parmesan	
(hard rind)	

Starchy foods (twice a week)

Allowed	**Not allowed**
Brown rice	Crisps
Bulgar wheat	Potatoes
Couscous	White rice
Dried peas	
Flageolet beans	
Haricot beans	
Kidney beans	
Lentils	
Pasta	
Polenta	
Split peas	

Meat (see the list on page 38 to which you can add)

Allowed	**Not allowed**
Cooked ham	Any fat around the ham
Leg of lamb	Cured ham
Pork fillet	Cuts from along the pork spine
	Fatty bits from the leg of lamb (outer slice)

Managing
celebration meals

So now you will be able to eat a good meal twice a week with, as you know, complete freedom. Take note, this does not mean 'celebration day', but 'celebration meal'. During these two meals you may eat any type of food, in particular those you have most missed during the diet's first two phases.

Get yourself organized

Your celebration meal can be either of the day's two main meals, but dinner is a better choice so that you have enough time to enjoy it and avoid bringing along any work stress that would stop you from enjoying every last mouthful. Plan your week. If you are invited out or if you have friends coming at the weekend, then decide to have your two celebration meals on these two days when you are relaxing. However, do ensure that the timing for these two meals is not too close.

Two conditions

You are allowed everything, but:

• you must never take second helpings
• you must never eat two celebration meals in sucession

Get into the routine of fitting a Phase 3 meal in between. If, for example, you have your first celebration meal at Tuesday lunchtime, then you must not have your second one on Tuesday evening.

You are allowed everything, but only one unit:

• one starter
• one main dish
• one dessert or cheese
• one glass of wine

Curry? Paella? Chocolate cake? You choose your menu, but just one serving of each course.

Be careful with apéritifs; if you have drunk a glass of champagne while chatting before the meal, then you are not allowed any wine during the meal.

Know how to 'shut the door again' after a celebration meal

Contrary to what you might think, the risk from these two moments of pleasure does not lie in what makes up the actual celebration meal, but rather in what you eat at your next meal when you have to be restricted again by certain limitations. The simplest way to tackle this is to bear this fact in mind. Write it down in your diary for the days following celebration meals so that you programme yourself to slip back into the Consolidation phase without any problem.

Give yourself some pleasure!

These two unrestricted menus also allow you to learn about pleasure, which you will need to learn how to control again. If before your diet you had the unfortunate habits of snacking in front of the television or scoffing whole jars of spread, these two meals are there to introduce you to a quite different form of pleasure. Savour, chew slowly, take your time and think about what you are eating. Pleasure and gluttony are two totally different ways of appreciating food. Here we want to open the door to pleasure and not to taking in food in a chaotic fashion. If you eat compulsively, this is bound to ruin your diet in the long term.

Two tips to stop yourself from taking seconds

• In a restaurant, your plate is brought to you with all the trimmings, vegetables etc. You do not ask for a second helping. Behave at home as if you were in a restaurant. Fill up your plate, but don't take any seconds.

• You can serve everything out onto individual plates so that you avoid bringing the whole dish to the table.

Pure protein
Thursdays

Throughout this day, you will only eat proteins that are as pure as possible, as if you were in Phase 1 of your diet. So the list of foods you are allowed is the Phase 1 list (see page 38).

Why choose Thursdays?

I chose Thursdays randomly. If Thursdays simply do not suit you because of the way your work is organized or eating pure proteins is likely to prove difficult on that day, you may select a different day, but make sure you decide upon a day once and for all and that you stick to it. If your pure proteins day becomes a moveable feast, then the whole Consolidation phase will be at risk.

And if I haven't been able to stick to my protein Thursday?

It may so happen that on one particular week the diet becomes impossible, but make sure this does not turn into a habit. If you were unable to keep to it, then make up for this the following day. However, be aware that it is only a short step from shifting the day around to giving up altogether. Another solution would be to anticipate any problem. If you can see from your diary that a Thursday is taken up with a business lunch or dinner with friends, then schedule your protein day for the Wednesday. This way you are still in control of your diet schedule. But here again, remember that your body loves habit and hates unpredictability. The more regular your eating patterns are throughout your week, the less risk you run with regard to the well-known rebound effect that we talked about on page 87.

Why is this day so crucial?

The Consolidation phase is a tricky one. The rebound effect can occur at any moment until such time as you have got through this phase, which will be that much longer if you have lost a lot of weight. This protein day acts like a rampart, protecting you against the rebound effect, and it helps you to stabilize your weight. So it is not under any circumstances negotiable. Do not forget that this Consolidation period is a phase when your body will react in an extreme way. If you make the slightest false move, the rebound effect will come into play. Pure protein Thursdays keep you safe.

Thursdays, for life

You might as well come to terms with this here and now as we will see in the Stabilization phase, pure protein Thursdays are the only non-negotiable instruction that you will have to stick to forever once you have finished this book and ended your diet. You have been overweight and your body remembers this. For the time being, let's say that your body is 'on probation'. Later on, in the Stabilization phase, you will be free to eat again as you want to, but you should never forget that for a period in your life your body has been different. These Thursdays are going to enable you to live normally, to avoid putting weight back on and to eat like everyone else. However, you might as well resign yourself to this now, Thursdays will not disappear from your horizon because they support and watch over those pounds from your past.

Think fish!

Fish contains fewer calories than meat. In fact, lean fish, such as sole, hake, cod, coley and skate have only 100 calories per 100g, whereas the leanest beef still provides 160 calories. As for the fattiest fish, such as salmon and mackerel, they do not exceed 200 calories, while fatty meat contains around 340 calories and certain cuts of pork even as much as 480 calories. The fattiest fish therefore often provides fewer calories than an ordinary beef steak. Because of this, fish is particularly recommended for weight-loss diets, as long as it is never fried, since this sends the calories soaring.

SOME SAMPLE MENUS FOR PHASE 3 (CONSOLIDATION)

	Aubergine and tofu lasagne (see page 198)	Strawberry and vanilla puddings (see page 246)	Chicken and prawns in a spicy coconut sauce (see page 210)
	MONDAY	**TUESDAY**	**WEDNESDAY**
Breakfast	>Hot drink >2 slices of wholemeal bread >1 fat-free yoghurt	>Hot drink >Dukan sandwich bread (see page 194) >Slices of lean chicken	>Hot drink >2 slices of wholemeal bread >Fat-free yoghurt
Lunch	>Tzatziki (Greek cucumber and yoghurt dip) with crudités >Roast pork fillet with braised fennel >Cheese	CELEBRATION MEAL >Creamy garlic mushrooms >Fish and chips >Chocolate fondant pudding >Wine (1 glass)	>Oat bran galette (see page 42) with smoked salmon and a dill and crème fraîche (3% fat) dip >Squashes stuffed with veal Bolognese (see page 192) and melted cheese >Rhubarb compote (see page 232)
Snack	> Slices of lean chicken + Dukan sandwich bread (see page 194)	>A cheese and salad sandwich (made with 2 slices of wholemeal bread)	>Crudités
Dinner	>Carrot salad with an orange and lemon juice dressing >Aubergine and tofu lasagne (see page 198) >Vanilla-hazelnut crème brûlée with strawberries (see page 238)	>Tomato and basil salad >Coconut chicken with French beans and tofu (see page 208) >Strawberry and vanilla puddings (see page 246)	>Hard-boiled quail's eggs with Dukan mayonnaise or celery salt >Chicken and prawns in a spicy coconut sauce (see page 210) >Lemon and lime meringue mousses (see page 236)

Do not forget your 2 tablespoons of oat bran, every day.

Scrambled egg with salmon roe (see page 134)	Floating islands with a hint of mocha (see page 250)	Normandy-style coquilles Saint-Jacques (see page 206)	Vanilla panna cotta with raspberries and balsamic syrup (see page 244)

THURSDAY (PP)	FRIDAY	SATURDAY	SUNDAY
>Hot drink >Lean ham >1 oat bran galette (see page 42)	>Hot drink >Bresaola >Fat-free yoghurt	>Hot drink >Oven-roasted tomatoes and mushrooms >Slices of lean turkey	>Hot drink >2 slices of wholemeal bread >Scrambled eggs
>Scrambled egg with salmon roe (see page 134) >Salmon and lemon slices baked in foil >Fat-free natural yoghurt with a sprinkling of cinnamon	>Soft-boiled egg with asparagus 'soliders' >Curried chicken club sandwich (see page 194) >Apricot clafoutis (see page 240)	>Cream of courgette soup >Normandy-style coquilles Saint-Jacques (see page 206) >Cinnamon apple surprise (see page 252)	>Grilled prawns marinated in tandoori spices and yoghurt with a fresh mint yoghurt raita >Chicken and vegetable curry (see page 204 and serve without the apple) >Brown rice >Vanilla panna cotta (see page 244)
>Seafood sticks	>2 slices of wholemeal bread	>Porridge (made from 2 tablespoons oat bran)	>1 oat bran galette (see page 42)
>Bresaola >Seafood poached in fish stock with saffron and a garlicky Dukan mayonnaise >Muesli ice cream (see page 214)	>Pumpkin loaf (see page 168) >Pasta with a spicy tomato sauce and shavings of Parmesan >Floating islands with a hint of mocha (see page 250)	CELEBRATION MEAL >Champagne (1 glass) >Garlic bread >Lasagne >Vanilla ice cream with a dark chocolate sauce	>Summer seafood surprise (see page 160) >Oven-roasted sea bass with chargrilled baby vegetables >Iced crème anglais (see page 238 and serve without the pineapple)

Fitting your diet into your daily life (Phase 3)

Eating with your family

At last you are allowed to eat pasta, bread and fruit, so it is easier for you to join in with family meals. As long as you stick to the quantities, you can eat like everyone else, or just about. Serve the pasta onto your plate before the others so that you make sure you do not exceed the quantities allowed. Of course, you will not take any second helpings. If your children are fed up with tomato sauce on their pasta, it is easy enough to provide two separate sauces and everyone can just help themselves. Go ahead and put some olive oil or fresh butter out on the table, this way you will get your children used to new tastes that are excellent for their health. As for you, have your spices at the ready!

Apéritif time

It is true that you are allowed one portion of cheese a day, two slices of bread and two servings of starchy foods a week in the Consolidation phase. But when you are having an apéritif, keeping a tally of everything you eat becomes impossible. How many cheese cubes can you eat? How many canapés are equivalent to a slice of bread? It is not worth trying to work it all out. Keep these 'extras' you are allowed (bread, starchy foods etc) for calm and regular times. You can decide, for example, that you will let yourself have your bread in the mornings for breakfast or at lunch with a soup. For apéritifs, as with the restaurant, put yourself back into Phase 2, that is proteins + vegetables. That way you won't run the risk of making mistakes. You can have cherry tomatoes, seafood sticks, crunchy vegetable pieces, sparkling water and Diet Coke.

Remember that while you are laughing and chatting with friends over an apéritif, you are not able to keep track of what you are eating. Getting embroiled in some complex calculation is dangerous as you are likely to spoil your evening and jeopardize your diet.

At the restaurant

So that you don't get misled, when you are in a restaurant think back to the proteins + vegetables phase as it is really difficult to stick to your instructions and take the new foods you are allowed into consideration while you are chatting away to friends. Do not allow yourself to be served any bread or pasta. It will be white bread and as for the pasta, it will not come with a sauce you want. If you think proteins + vegetables when you choose from the menu, you won't have any problem. Smoked salmon, for example, is an all-purpose dish you can order almost anywhere. As for an accompaniment, you can always opt for French beans and spinach or a salad.

Wine, bread and dessert are not allowed, unless you have decided to make this trip to the restaurant a celebration meal. If it is a celebration, order one glass of wine. In a restaurant, you cannot have seconds, which is an advantage since this is one of your instructions for the celebration meals. As for the other days, you have to learn to say no to yourself and order a coffee instead of dessert. Don't forget that you are allowed Diet Coke – it will help you do without sugary flavours.

For a happy diet, follow François Mauriac's example

The French writer, François Mauriac, frail and anything but athletic, adopted the habit of jumping up and down in front of a full-length mirror. He started off with small, gentle bends to get his legs warmed up, then gradually he jumped higher and higher. I thought this was a fantastic idea so I tried it out myself. I started jumping, as he suggested, when I felt joy, and I noticed that this exercise made my joy more intense!

I eventually realized that joy, which by definition is ephemeral, lasted longer with this physical exertion. So I then tested out jumping like this in isolation without connecting it with joy. And I became aware that jumping gave me joy.

Since then, I have been finding little moments of joy for myself and I keep the connection going in both directions.

And at the same time, I am developing my quadriceps, the muscles that use up the most calories, and I am controlling my weight.

Questions and answers

Why do I have to count five days for every pound lost?

→ Why five days and not four or three? When I devised my first Attack diet, I achieved results that were spectacular, but short-lived. The pounds people lost tended to go back on again. So I introduced new foods, while continuing to supervise and control. When I checked through all my statistics on weight regain with a statistician, I saw that Consolidation phases were always successful when based on five days for every pound lost.

Why reintroduce wholemeal bread rather than white bread?

→ White bread is not a natural food because of the way it is made, from flour where the wheat has been artificially separated from its husk, the bran. It is a food that is too easily assimilated and is quickly digested. It does not provide you with all the goodness you get from wholemeal bread.

→ Wholemeal or wholewheat bread contains a natural proportion of bran and the wheatgerm is also intact. Bran protects you from bowel cancer, excess cholesterol, diabetes, constipation and, given what we are interested in here, it also looks after your figure. Once it reaches your small intestine, the bran sticks together, trapping some calories that get eliminated along with the stools without your body absorbing them. Wholemeal bread also takes much longer to digest, as well as making you feel satiated.

Can I eat low-fat cheeses?

→ You can, but most low-fat cheeses are of no interest to the taste buds and you will be tempted to eat more than you should.

How can I stop smoking and follow the diet at the same time without feeling too much frustration?

→ Giving up smoking is so important for looking after your health that once you have made up your mind, it is right to give this absolute priority. So if you have to make a choice, you must put giving up smoking before losing weight. If you want to do everything at once, this is possible, but managing both successfully is rare. You must give up smoking completely and separately for ten days. From the eleventh day onwards, you can then tackle your weight at the same time. To avoid being overwhelmed by the frustrations of doing both, you must make full use of one of the Dukan Diet's main advantages as it allows you complete freedom of quantities. Whenever you are gasping for a cigarette, you can eat as much as you want from the list of allowed foods.

Are my thyroid problems compatible with your diet?

→ In the battle to prevent people from becoming overweight, the thyroid and thyroid problems pose quite a problem. Firstly, there are people who, unaware of having a thyroid insufficiency or just a lazy thyroid, gradually gain weight. By the time they have found this out, the extra pounds are well established.

→ There are also people who have been diagnosed with a thyroid deficiency. They are given Levothyroxine replacement therapy, but often this takes a long time to take effect so the body continues storing away extra pounds.

→ Some doctors are wary, preferring to take their time with diagnosis and treatment, whereas all this does is allow extra time for weight to accumulate. Even for those people with an insufficiency who are quickly diagnosed and properly treated, it should not be forgotten that what Levothyroxine gives them is not identical to what their thyroid produced.

→ Think of the difference between ready-to-wear and made-to-measure clothing. This is just to make you aware of the complexity of the problem. If a person wants to lose weight, with the right treatment that fits in with how their thyroid function is progressing, they will lose weight, that I can assure you. However, let's say that people with thyroid problems must be taken a little more seriously than others, just a little more seriously, but no more.

Phase 3 summary

Do not neglect this stage

During stages 1 and 2, you found positive encouragement every day as you could see from your scales that your weight was dropping. In the Consolidation phase, your weight no longer drops so it is easy to drift and consider skipping this stage. Whatever you do, don't put this book down! You are only halfway there! If you ignore the instructions in this phase, your pounds are bound to pile back on, and very quickly too.

Remain vigilant – the success of your diet depends on this Consolidation phase

You may react in another way by following the Consolidation phase, but only half-heartedly: an extra slice of bread here, another piece of fruit there, three celebration meals instead of two and so on. Remain vigilant and, most importantly, be totally objective about what you do eat. Some people on the diet are surprised to see their scales go up 'when they had been following the instructions'. If you are afraid of making this mistake, write down all the foods you are allowed in a little notebook and also note down everything you have eaten in the day. Be completely honest with yourself. Don't leave out any of your little snacks if you were unable to resist a food you are not allowed.

Tell yourself that this is your last diet

Going on diets one after the other is bad for two reasons:

• First of all, your body gets used to successive diets. It soon notices any attempts to restrict intake and so it immediately sets about better managing its reserves! A person who sheds weight and then puts it back on again several times in their life, becomes vaccinated against losing weight. After each time that they fail, they will find it more difficult to lose weight again. Your body keeps a record of previous diets. So if you have kept going right up to the Consolidation phase, stick with the diet until the very end, telling yourself that this is the last diet you will ever embark on.

• But that is not all. Did you know that when you are dieting the fats you eliminate move around in your body? Once you have lost a stone or two, it is a little like having eaten a stone or two of butter or lard! A great quantity of cholesterol and triglycerides is moving around in your blood and these toxic fats can block up the arteries. This is why losing weight, regaining it, then losing it again is a complete disaster for your health. The risk you run from having fats circulating in your blood is of course largely outweighed by the benefits you gain from losing weight. However, be aware of the repercussions this may have on your health if you go through this process more than twice in your life.

Take heart!

The time you spend dieting will quickly go by. Whereas a great figure, will stay with you for a long time. This summary page devoted to Phase 3 is particularly important as you must be totally prepared psychologically to start on this part of the diet. Whether you succeed in losing weight depends on this.

The Consolidation phase in a nutshell

Five days for every pound lost.
How long the Consolidation phase lasts depends on how much weight you have lost. This phase is not optional. It is compulsory and non-negotiable.

Keep your base of proteins + vegetables, as much as you want.

And add:
- one portion of fruit per day (except for bananas, grapes and cherries)
- two slices of wholemeal bread per day
- 40g (1 $^1/_2$ oz) cheese per day

Go walking every day
and look for any possible opportunity to incorporate exercise into your daily routine.

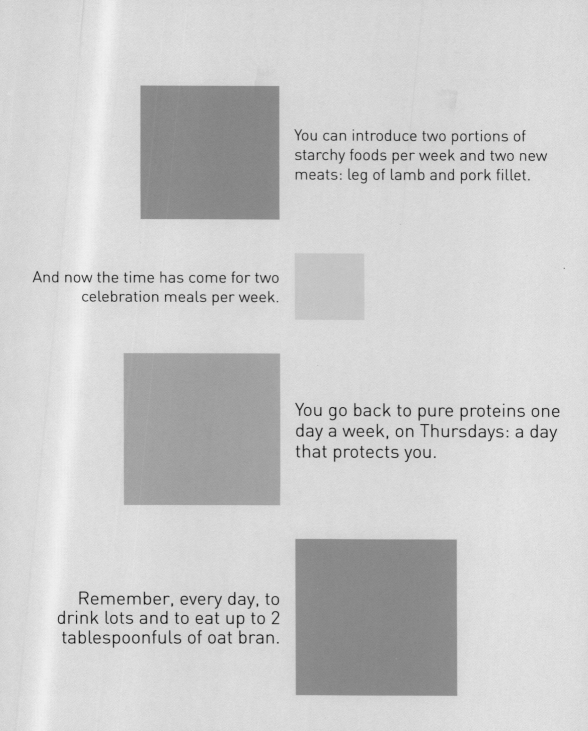

You can introduce two portions of starchy foods per week and two new meats: leg of lamb and pork fillet.

And now the time has come for two celebration meals per week.

You go back to pure proteins one day a week, on Thursdays: a day that protects you.

Remember, every day, to drink lots and to eat up to 2 tablespoonfuls of oat bran.

Phase 4:
Permanent Stabilization

The Stabilization phase: a new life protected by three simple, concrete, but non-negotiable measures.

What you are aiming
for in Phase 4

Freedom again

First of all, well done! If you are reading these pages, this is because you have successfully got through the trickiest stages of our diet. By this point you have not only got rid of your extra pounds, but you have also safely navigated the difficult days in Consolidation, a phase when your body was likely to play tricks on you. Today any danger of the dreaded rebound effect is past. You will be able once again to eat more spontaneously, without any great risk of regaining weight. You have had to follow many instructions, some more restrictive than others. These instructions were there to guide you – a lighthouse in the storm. Now you will be able to sail far away from the shores, but we will leave you three compasses on board: three simple, concrete, easy, but non-negotiable instructions.

Permanent Stabilization, instructions for the very long term

In theory, you are going to be able to eat freely. In practice, I have to add a few qualifications here and some extra explanations. Yes, from now on everything will be possible for you. I mean that in theory there is no longer anything that you are not allowed. But you will have to adopt three keys measures because without them, you will be on a slope and gravity being what it is, you will end up slipping down. Here are the three measures that you will have to abide by every week, for as long as you want to maintain this new weight that you have worked so hard to attain:

• You will keep to protein Thursdays.
• You will never again take lifts or escalators. You will walk up the stairs.
• You will eat 3 tablespoonfuls of oat bran every day.

As for everything else, it is vital that you keep in mind what you have learnt along your journey. Stage by stage, you have moved from vital foods to pleasurable foods and now you know how to correctly prioritize these foods. Maintain this habit.

Have confidence in yourself

The great difference between Stabilization and Consolidation is your independence. Today you have regained your independence and you are in control of operations. Do not underestimate yourself. Today you are capable of going it alone. As your diet progressed, the difficult days included, you and your body learnt a great deal – the four stages in this diet have enabled you to develop in-depth knowledge about how to eat. You can now differentiate between what is important and what is superfluous. Starting with the protein diet, you discovered the power of these vital foods. You then continued onwards, adding indispensable vegetables to this base and lastly, in the Consolidation phase, you were able to discriminate and complete your menus with important foods (fruit), useful foods (wholemeal bread), then comfort foods (starchy foods) and finally pleasurable foods (cheese and celebration meals) and dangerous foods (nuts, spreads, crisps and mayonnaise etc). Your body has grown accustomed to eating in a different way. From now on, you can trust it and give it the freedom it deserves.

Do not confuse Stabilization with Consolidation

Perhaps you leafed through the pages of this book a little too quickly, thinking that Stabilization and Consolidation were two similar things. If this is the case, then go back quickly, otherwise your diet will be at risk. In the Stabilization phase, the restrictions are very insignificant since the dieters who reach this phase have got past the well-known rebound effect. In the Consolidation phase, everything is devised so as to remove any risk of you putting weight back on. This is not so in the Stabilization period as the risk has now been eliminated.

The three rules you have to keep to for a very long time

Why not forever!

A protein Thursday every week

From now on you are free to eat normally six days out of seven, but this final permanent instruction will be all that protects you from your tendency to put weight back on. During this day, you will select the purest possible proteins. You may also use powdered proteins (but not just any old powder), if this helps you. As with the Consolidation phase, this instruction is of course non-negotiable – you must persevere with the habit you acquired during your diet. Choose your day and stick to it. If you keep on shifting it around, you will forget about this day, and slowly but surely you will put weight back on.

A major contract: giving up lifts and escalators

If you are not sporty, do not take any lifts and escalators and avoid using your car for very short journeys: in other words, get yourself moving! To motivate yourself, you can buy yourself a pedometer to count the number of steps you take each day. You will soon notice that if you lead a sedentary life, they will not amount to much. So, without turning into a top-level athlete, get your legs working every day as part of your daily routine.

3 tablespoonfuls of oat bran per day

Oat bran offers you three major benefits:
• it aids digestion and protects your intestines from serious illnesses;
• when part of the bolus, it prevents the small intestine from absorbing all the calories in your food;
• in your stomach, oat bran increases in volume and it gives you a pleasant feeling of satiety.
Eating oat bran daily is beneficial for your health and will ensure that your newly rediscovered figure is long-lived.

Should I opt for
foods with reduced fat
and sugar?

Reduced-fat foods

Nowadays, nobody would dispute the value of reduced-fat foods. There is clear evidence that people do not eat more of them to compensate for their low fat content. In practice, the foods that have most gained from a reduction in their fat content are semi-skimmed milk, now used routinely even for children, fromage frais and yoghurts, of which natural yoghurt, the most widely sold, is a semi-skimmed product anyway. Other reduced-fat foods, such as butter, cheese, sauces and cooked meat products, are of more value to people on a restricted diet or at risk of cardiovascular disease. Excess fat also seems to be a factor that increases the risk of various cancers, such as breast, colon, prostate, pancreas and ovarian.

Reduced-sugar foods

The benefit of these is less clear-cut. It seems that the body can partly detect artificial sugars and to compensate it eats more, so that a taste for sugar continues to be fuelled and even stimulated. However, it has been proven that this compensation is never total and it gradually diminishes with use, especially among adults.

Nowadays, the foods that are of most benefit to the obese and diabetics are aspartame, diet fizzy drinks and proper sugar-free chewing gum. Apart from these particular examples, whatever the type of food, the reduced sugar content is aimed far more at people who want to avoid putting on weight than at those who are trying to lose weight.

Some reduced-fat foods

FAT CONTENT (CALORIES/100G)

FOOD	NORMAL	LOW-FAT
Butter	758	450
Camembert	283	236
Cubes of bacon/pancetta	280	261
Emmental cheese	400	216
Ham	169	110
Margarine	758	450
Mayonnaise	710	396
Vinaigrette	658	323
Yoghurt (full-fat or 0% fat, 125g/4½oz pot)	90	45

Protein Thursdays

A little reminder

Try to avoid mustard now on Thursdays as it is salty. Instead, season as you want, using vinegar, pepper and herbs. To make up for this deprivation, muster up all your spices.

Cutting down lactose

Now that your permanent Stabilization diet occurs just one day a week, your proteins have to be very carefully selected and your lactose intake should be reduced. When the composition of low-fat yoghurt and low-fat fromage frais is compared, you will notice that for the same number of calories, fromage frais provides more protein and less lactose than yoghurt.

Selecting very pure proteins

Protein Thursdays are a small, weekly reminder of the 'Attack' period, with a few slight differences. You will therefore have to maintain the habits you acquired in Phase 1 when choosing pure proteins. For example, as far as meat goes, you will avoid pork and lamb since they are far too fatty to be considered as pure proteins. On page 116, you have a definitive list of the foods allowed on protein Thursdays. Indeed, given that this Thursday is all that is left to protect you from any possible weight regain, it is important that you select the purest possible proteins. Oily fish was allowed as part of your Attack diet, but here it will be banned on Thursdays.

Drink lots

In the Attack phase, we recommended that you drink at last 1.5 litres of water a day. For these stabilizing Thursdays, we advise you to increase the dose and drink 2 litres a day, so that your body can really clean out its system.

Cut down on salt

The whole time you are losing weight and consolidating, the Dukan Diet only stipulates cutting down salt. For the Stabilization phase Thursdays, this instruction will be stepped up, as now there must be much less salt on this 'protection' day.

Being limited to an occasional single day, this restriction is not enough to lower your blood pressure, but it will allow the water that you take in to pass quickly through your body and cleanse it out. This instruction will be of particular benefit to women who are strongly influenced by their hormones, which cause massive water retention throughout their cycles.

You are allowed powdered proteins occasionally

Since the Dukan Diet is completely natural, until now powdered proteins have been forbidden. Even though this is an artificial way of eating, powdered proteins do have the advantage of being particularly pure. In the Stabilization phase, once the diet only takes up one day a week, it is possible to make use of them, especially if you are travelling or if a busy workload means you risk missing a protein Thursday. As they come in powder form, they are definitely easy to carry around with you. However, you must not lose sight of the fact that these are artificial foods. Your body is not naturally programmed to feed itself with powder. Even when it is flavoured and sweetened, powder is not a pleasurable food. Prolonged use of these products is likely to lead you into uncontrollable episodes of bulimia. What's more, as these mixes contain no fibre whatsoever, they may cause unpleasant abdominal bloating. So you must only ever eat them very occasionally.

If you do buy powder, be careful not to mistake meal replacements for powdered proteins. Read the labels carefully. Any powder you choose must be made up of at least 95% protein.

A few tips

• **If you like beef**
On Thursdays, beef benefits from being cooked sufficiently. This does not alter the quality of its proteins, but it does get rid of a greater part of the fat.

• **Leave the salmon for another day!**
In the Phase 1 pure protein diet, all fish are allowed, from the leanest to the oiliest. In the Stabilization phase, their fat content means that oily fish is no longer permissible for protein Thursdays.

• **Think raw fish!**
This is an ideal way of preparing fish such as monkfish, sea bream and coley. Cut the very fresh raw fish up into small cubes or very thin slices and marinate for a few minutes in lemon juice, adding salt, black pepper and herbes de Provence, and you will have created a quick and delicious meal.

What can you eat
on protein Thursdays?

Thursdays must be strictly protein only. Use foods with the purest possible proteins. You cannot go back to the Attack diet list. Certain proteins that were allowed then, are now no longer permitted on these protein Thursdays. Here is the list of pure proteins you are allowed.

Meat

Allowed
Beef steak/Minced steak (max. 5% fat content)
Fillet of beef
Roast beef
Veal escalope/Roast veal (well cooked)
Rabbit
Cooked ham slices
Fat-reduced bacon

Not allowed
Sirloin steak
Lamb
Rib of beef
Rib-eye steak
Pork
Veal chop

Eggs

Allowed
Hen's eggs (whole or just the whites if you have eaten heavily that week)

Poultry

Allowed
Chicken breast (without the skin)
Upper part of chicken drumsticks (without the skin)
Guinea fowl
Pigeon
Quail
Turkey

Not allowed
Duck
Goose
Chicken skin
Chicken wings
Chicken – parson's nose

Dairy products

Allowed
Fat-free Greek yoghurt/Fat-free natural yoghurt (plain or flavoured with aspartame)
Fat-free fromage frais
Not allowed
Cheese
Whole milk dairy products

Fish

Allowed
Cod (fresh)/Ling
Dab/Lemon sole
Dover sole
Grey mullet
Hake
Halibut
Monkfish
Plaice
Pollock/Coley
Red mullet
Sea bass
Sea bream
Seafood sticks (surimi)
Skate
Swordfish
Tuna (and tinned tuna in water/brine)
Turbot
Whiting

Not allowed
Mackerel
Sardines
Salmon
Smoked salmon (and smoked trout, haddock and eel)
Tinned tuna in oil

Shellfish

Allowed
Crab
Mussels
Oysters
Prawns
Scallops

SOME SAMPLE MENUS FOR PHASE 4 (STABILIZATION)

Lemon and lime meringue mousses (see page 230)

Red mullet fillets with basil (see page 206)

Spicy compote (see page 242)

	MONDAY	TUESDAY	WEDNESDAY
Breakfast	>Hot drink >Swedish crispbread >Butter >Cottage cheese	>Hot drink >Scrambled eggs >Cooked ham	>Hot drink >Slices of toast and butter >1 yoghurt >Fruit
Lunch	>Grated carrot salad >Sausages with lentils >Cheese >Strawberry and vanilla puddings (see page 246)	>Avocado with crab >Red mullet fillets with basil (see page 202) >Ice cream	>Tabouleh >Seafood sauerkraut (see page 176) >Pineapple with iced crème anglaise (see page 238)
Snack	>1 fruit	>Biscuits	>1 fruit
Dinner	>Cucumber with yoghurt and garlic >Pasta with a courgette sauce >Lemon and lime meringue mousses (see page 232)	>Lamb's lettuce salad >Vegetarian pizza >1 fruit	>Baby leeks in vinaigrette >Lasagne >Spicy compote (see page 242)

Do not forget your 3 tablespoons of oat bran, every day.

Spicy omelette with fresh mint (see page 172)

Cinnamon apple surprise (see page 252)

Gingerbread (see page 224)

Apricot clafoutis (see page 240)

THURSDAY (PP)	FRIDAY	SATURDAY	SUNDAY
>Hot drink >Fat-free fromage frais >1 oat bran galette (see page 42)	>Hot drink >Cereal and milk >Fruit	>Hot drink >Slices of toast and butter >Jam or marmalade	>Hot drink >Orange juice >Croissant
>Hard-boiled eggs >Steak tartare >Muesli ice cream (see page 214)	>Poached egg and bacon salad >Slow-cooked beef with red wine and shallots >Gratin dauphinois >Mixed fruit salad	>Mixed green salad >Chicken and chips >Gingerbread (see page 224)	>Tomato and mozzarella salad >Roast loin of lamb >French beans >Apricot clafoutis (see page 240)
>Seafood sticks	>1 yoghurt	>1 oat bran galette (see page 42)	>Fruit yoghurt
>Spicy omelette with fresh mint (see page 172) >Grilled sea bass >Fat-free yoghurt	>Asparagus >Grilled chicken breast >Ratatouille >Cinnamon apple surprise (see page 252)	>Warm goat's cheese on a bed of rocket >Chicken and lime kebabs >Fried courgettes >Tiramisu	>Vegetable soup >Herby omelette >1 fruit

Fitting your protein Thursdays into
your daily life (Phase 4)

What's this? Are you still dieting?

If you did not notice it before, you are bound to be aware now how, as soon as you start dieting, everyone around you is forever encouraging you to break your rules, using the usual excuse, 'Go on, treat yourself!' Food has always been a sensitive topic of conversation. What we choose to eat represents at the same time our culture, our convictions and our childhood memories etc. If you managed to avoid this sort of remark when you were dieting, you are likely to face a barrage now that you are no longer on a diet. Yet, every Thursday, you are going to eat differently to everyone else.

Two solutions for dealing with reactions from the people around you:
• You take ownership and silence any remarks. The way you eat is your business and no one else's. It does not bother anyone and you are not stopping other people from eating.
• You keep quiet about it. You are not going to explain the Dukan method to your boss at work or to the client you have invited to a restaurant for a business lunch.

Here are a few tips...

Eating with your family

Have brunch once a week. Your protein day could be the ideal opportunity for instigating a new family ritual and making your breakfast a bit special: eggs and cold meats, for you a brunch is perfect! Whereas the others will finish off their breakfast with toast and marmalade, nobody will notice you dipping chicken 'soldiers' into your soft-boiled egg!

At the restaurant
• **Order seafood**
There is something festive about eating seafood and no one will notice

you following your protein Thursday instructions. Did you know that crab, prawns, mussels, oysters and scallops too are even leaner than fish?

• Don't eat your plate clean
Order as large a piece as possible of grilled meat and ask to have this served without any vegetables or sauces.

• For dessert, order a coffee
If you order a coffee when the others choose a dessert, nobody will have an inkling that you are on a diet. If the conversation keeps going, then order yourself another one.

Travelling

Take some powdered protein with you. It is difficult to follow a protein diet at somewhere like a motorway service station, although if you are lucky in some you might find slices of cold meat. But if you cannot find anything appropriate when you're on the road, then you can make do with powdered protein and complete your meal with a low-fat dairy product if you can find one.

Questions and answers

In the mornings I take the pill along with my oat bran. Should I take them separately?

→ It all depends on how much oat bran you eat. One or two tablespoonfuls of bran are not enough to stop your pill from working, even if it is a low-dose pill. If you have three spoonfuls and your pill is an ultra low-dose, then take it in the evening. If it is a normal dose pill, it does not matter, you can take them together.

Can you suggest a food that will suppress my appetite?

→ Aubergines can be a good natural appetite suppressant. Take a good-sized aubergine and, using a knife with a sharp point, prick it three times on each side, making 1cm (½ inch) deep slits, and push a garlic clove into each one. Bake the aubergine in the oven at 240°C/475°F/Gas 9.

→ Once you hear the skin hiss as it starts to crack and open up, remove the aubergine and transfer it to a plate. Then cut it in two, lengthways, as you would an avocado.

→ Take one half, add salt and black pepper, and eat the flesh with a small spoon as if it were an ice cream. Once you have finished, try sitting down to eat. Feelings of satisfaction and satiety will both be working their way to your brain. You will be much calmer as you eat your lunch or dinner. The pectin in the aubergine offers further help, as it takes away a few calories with it when it leaves your body.

What is the best time of day to eat the bran?

→ There are several different options, depending on your lifestyle and your relationship to food.

→ If you are a morning person who enjoys a hearty breakfast, it is clear you will find it substantial, soothing and filling, especially if you make galettes, crêpes or porridge with the bran.

→ If you are a late afternoon snacker, then the best time for you would be five o'clock.

→ If you grab a quick snack for lunch and never have time to make a proper meal, a large galette made from 2 tablespoonfuls of bran, fromage frais and an egg white can be used to make a Dukan sandwich filled with a nice slice of smoked salmon, some lean ham or bresaola.

→ If you are a person who snacks after dinner and rifles empty cupboards vainly searching for a treat, a sweet galette with some reduced-fat cocoa powder is the best idea to prevent you from succumbing.

Phase 4 summary

Those who take it slow and steady, go a long way

So here you are at the end of this journey to the centre of your body. You gave it a hard time, you waged war on it, but now you can set off again, hand in hand. Your body is your friend; learn how to pay it proper attention. According to an old saying, 'He who takes it slow and steady, goes a long way.' And today there are many of us who unfortunately spend far more time worrying about the state of their car and whether it is working properly, than they do about their own body. We would not dream of putting ordinary petrol in a diesel engine or of not bothering to take our precious car for a service or oil change.

Think about yourself

For this diet to be permanently successful, you will need to think about yourself every day. When you were losing weight, you devoted time to your body. You listened to it, you pampered it or treated it harshly, but you paid it attention. You are going to have to continue in this vein. This is why Thursdays are an important day. This day is a rallying point for you and your body, a time to reexamine your relationship.

Become a tortoise at mealtimes

Taking care of your body means giving yourself some pleasure. Eat slowly, savour your food and don't swallow anything down without having appreciated it fully. Insist on this as doing things slowly is a way of life that nowadays is dying out. The more rapidly people eat, the more weight they put on.

Don't have seconds

You learnt about this in the Consolidation phase for your celebration meals. Take your time, but never take second helpings. One last piece of advice, which goes some way to helping you rediscover pleasure in eating as well as in your figure, is to eat with a knife and fork. Rather peculiar advice? Today, all our snacking and fast food has made us forget what is so obvious. If you take the time to enjoy a meal sitting down with a knife and fork, you are bound to relish what you are eating instead of scoffing whatever is available through the day.

Drink while you are eating

The idea that this is wrong still persists. However, drinking while you eat does your body absolutely no harm whatsoever. Drinking makes you feel satiated and it also means that the absorption of solid foods gets interrupted, which slows down the meal as it works its way through the gastrointestinal tract. Furthermore, cold water lowers the temperature of any food ingested, which gives the body extra work. And the harder it works, the more calories it uses up.

If you start to put a few pounds back on...

Do something before too many go back on. As soon as you start regaining any weight, over just one week try eating pure proteins for two days and that should be all you need.

Now, I am sure that you are well enough equipped to face up to the challenge that awaits you as you put this book down, which is to live pleasantly, eating once and for all like everyone else six days out of seven. The life you used to have when you felt so uncomfortable in your own skin, is now behind you.

The Stabilization phase in a nutshell

Disregarding your Stabilization instructions is a sure-fire way of putting back on the weight you have lost.

You will eat normally six days out of seven, in the Stabilization phase.

You will try to apply what you have learnt during this diet. You will work out when to eat different foods, depending on how important they are: vital (proteins, vegetables), pleasant (carbohydrates), indispensable, useful, comforting or pleasurable.

Once a week, preferably on Thursdays, go back to pure proteins.

These instructions are non-negotiable.
They will act as your rampart against possibly regaining weight.

On Thursdays, you will drink at least 2 litres of water.

You will eat 3 tablespoonfuls of oat bran every day.

You will avoid taking lifts and escalators.
Every day, your body will have to be active, even if you are not sporty.

Two major advances that change everything:
personalization and monitoring

Personalization: an approach with a human face

• An international study

In 2003, I set up a network group to conduct an international study on the disturbing increase in weight problems and obesity across the world. Colleagues who are nutritionists in America, England, Spain and Germany were witnessing the spread of this scourge and searching for solutions.

One fact became obvious: up until then, nothing had managed to hold this weight problem epidemic in check. Opposition to it had been further weakened because research was carried out in isolation and one method, the low-calorie approach, had been chosen with general approval.

Another conclusion from the analysis highlighted that an underlying obstacle was the difficulty of dieting in a world that constantly encourages us to consume. To overcome this obstacle, help and supervision were required. This was based on two obvious elements: a personal relationship with the person who was going to put themselves through the restriction of dieting alongside daily monitoring to give them support, day after day, pound after pound.

• The internet, a medium for personalization

All the books, methods and plans put forward to deal with weight problems, whatever their merits, are standardized methods that do not take into account the individual and their personality, their family history and their eating preferences.

The 'mass personalization' project focused on creating a programme that would enable us to carry out a personalized study for each overweight individual. From the questions drawn up by a doctor and colleague, we were able to collect 154 answers to build a profile of an individual case.

Based on all the elements taken into consideration, a comprehensive weight-loss programme was suggested to fit with the individual's weight personality – a proper road map. This project drew upon the combined talents of 32 doctors and a team of computer engineers and resulted in us creating the first book in the history of publishing to be written for a single reader.

Based on 10,000 cases, the Apage study showed that treating weight problems using a personalized approach adds a new tool to our arsenal as we fight to eradicate these problems. Optimum weight loss matched that achieved using the best methods available, but the results were radically better for stabilizing weight and maintaining it over 24 months.

Daily monitoring: a pain control programme

• Coaching on the internet

Further international consensus focuses on how terribly important daily monitoring is and, as a rule, a qualified nutritionist takes on this role. However, in France, for example, there are only 270 nutritionists to look after 20 million overweight people. So a coaching system needed to be devised that could be used on a large scale. The only medium that could host such a system and facilitate dialogue was the internet.

Take care! There are many internet sites that offer coaching. As far as I know none of them, not even the biggest sites, provide a personalized service (they make no distinction between users) or proper monitoring (their standard instructions do not factor in results).

• Instructions in the morning, then report back in the evening

The same medical and clinical teams drew upon the expertise acquired from the previous personalization project to create a unique service based on new and patented technology: the daily to-and-fro email system.

Each morning an email is sent with instructions adapted to suit each user. There are three sections covering food (menus), exercise and motivational support and dialogue.

Each evening is when personalization comes into its own, along with the integrity of the monitoring, as the user reports back with a few clicks on their day's weight, their eating lapses, exercise, level of motivation and the food they have most missed. Lastly, proving that this monitoring is real, the information provided in the report is then taken into consideration to work out the instructions email for the following day.

It is this patient and constant supervision, through a daily to-ing and fro-ing of instructions and reporting back, that enables users to lose weight with the least frustration and the best results, which are then sustainable over the longest time.

In practice

Compiling and analysing the answers from a questionnaire with 154 questions means it is possible to explore and develop an individual's set of circumstances. A study is undertaken and, a week later, a summary is produced, published and one single copy is printed for the exclusive attention of the individual.

You can fill out the questionnaire on the internet at www.livredemonpoids.com

Internet coaching is available on www.dukandiet.co.uk.

Readers of this book can benefit from preferential access and prices by using the code 'Hodder'.

Starters and appetizers

PHASE 1/
PHASE 2
PP

Mini smoked salmon vol-au-vents

Mini-bouchées au saumon fumé

- **Makes approximately 50 vol-au-vents**
- **Preparation time**
  25 minutes
- **Cooking time**
  20 minutes
- **Ingredients**

For the vol-au-vent pastry
6 tablespoons oat bran
1 teaspoon baking powder
3 tablespoons virtually fat-free quark
3 eggs
1 egg white
1 teaspoon bitter almond flavouring (optional)
www.mydukandietshop.co.uk
Salt and black pepper

For the filling
100g (3½oz) fat-free fromage frais
3 teaspoons virtually fat-free quark
Fresh herbs, such as chives
2 large slices of smoked salmon
Salt and black pepper

Preheat the oven to 220°C/425°F/Gas 7.

In a bowl, mix together the bran, baking powder, quark, eggs, egg white and bitter almond flavouring. Season with a little salt and black pepper and bring the pastry together.

Divide the pastry into about 50 pieces and use them to fill a silicone mini tartlet mould. Bake, in batches if necessary, for 20 minutes. As cooking times vary from to oven to oven, keep a careful eye on the vol-au-vents.

In a bowl, mix together the fromage frais and quark. Use a fork to blend it all in smoothly, then add salt, black pepper and fresh herbs, such as some finely chopped chives, if you have them.

Using a small spoon or piping bag, pipe this mixture on top of the vol-au-vents.

Cut the salmon up into tiny squares and garnish the vol-au-vents. Decorate with more fresh herbs.

Instead of smoked salmon, you could also use lumpfish roe or substitute the fromage frais filling with a tuna, salmon or smoked tofu mousse.

In the Attack and Cruise phases, remember you should not eat more than 2 tablespoonfuls of oat bran per day.

Scrambled eggs with salmon roe

Œufs brouillés aux œufs de salmon

- **2 servings**
- **Preparation time**
  15 minutes
- **Cooking time**
  10 minutes
- **Refrigeration time**
  10 minutes
- **Ingredients**
  3 eggs
  2 teaspoons salmon roe
  Salt and black pepper
  For the creamy topping
  2 egg whites, beaten
  30g (1oz) virtually fat-free quark
  30g (1oz) fat-free fromage frais
  Salt and black pepper

Break the eggs into a small heavy-bottomed pan and add salt and black pepper. Cook over a very gentle heat, constantly stirring with a wooden spoon and drawing a figure of eight. Once the eggs are well scrambled with a creamy texture, put them into two small dishes.

To make the creamy topping, whisk the egg whites until very firm, then stir in the quark and fromage frais, salt and black pepper.

Pour the topping over the eggs and decorate with the salmon roe.

Refrigerate for 10 minutes or until ready to serve.

Tandoori tofu
Tofu tandoori

PHASE 1/ PHASE 2 PP

- **2 servings**
- **Preparation time**
  10 minutes
- **Refrigeration time**
  3 to 8 hours
- **Cooking time**
  25 minutes
- **Ingredients**
  1 tablespoon lemon juice
  150g (5½oz) fat-free natural yoghurt, well stirred
  2 tablespoons tandoori spice powder
  250g (9oz) firm tofu
  Salt and black pepper

Mix together the lemon juice, yoghurt and spice powder.

Cut the tofu into cubes and add to the yoghurt mixture. Stir it in really well so that the cubes are completely covered with the yoghurt mixture. Refrigerate for a few hours, or even better overnight.

Preheat the oven to 240°C/475°F/Gas 9.

Place the cubes in an ovenproof dish with the marinade. Bake in the oven for 25 minutes, turning them over at regular intervals.

Serve the cubes hot and with cocktail sticks if desired.

PHASE 2
PP

Mediterranean prawns in a vanilla sauce

Gambas en verrines dans leur sauce vanillée

- **4 servings**
- **Preparation time**
  15 minutes
- **Cooking time**
  20 minutes
- **Ingredients**
  1 vanilla pod
  150ml (5fl oz) crème fraîche (3% fat)
  (tolerated)
  2 shallots
  2 tablespoons white wine (optional
  and tolerated)
  12 Mediterranean prawns
  ½ teaspoon turmeric
  ¼ teaspoon paprika

Split the vanilla pod in half and scrape out the seeds. Heat the crème fraîche until it just starts to boil, then add the vanilla pod and seeds and leave to infuse.

Peel and finely chop the shallots and cook with 4 tablespoons water over a very gentle heat in a non-stick frying pan until they turn transparent. Pour in the white wine and reduce a little. Add the peeled prawns and gently pan-fry until just cooked through.

Pour in the crème fraîche (having first removed the vanilla pod) and sprinkle in the turmeric and paprika.

Transfer to four small dishes and serve hot.

PHASE 2
PP

Pan-fried scallops with a vanilla foam

Saint-jacques poêlées, vanille en écume

- **4 servings**
- **Preparation time**
  20 minutes
- **Cooking time**
  15 minutes
- **Ingredients**
  16 frozen scallops
  150ml (5fl oz) low-salt fish stock (tolerated)
  1 vanilla pod
  10 drops of white rum flavouring (optional)
  www.mydukandietshop.co.uk
  100ml (3½fl oz) crème fraîche (3% fat) (tolerated) or 100g (3½oz) fat-free fromage frais
  1 generous pinch of agar-agar

Thaw the scallops in the refrigerator.

Pour the stock into a saucepan. Split the vanilla pod lengthways, scraping the seeds into the stock. Bring to the boil and leave the pod to infuse for 10 minutes. Strain and keep the pod for decoration if you wish.

In a non-stick frying pan, gently brown the scallops for 2 to 3 minutes. Keep warm.

Deglaze the frying pan using 2 tablespoons water mixed with the rum flavouring. Stir in the fish stock. Add the crème fraîche, then the agar-agar and strain.

If you have a cream whipper, pour in the mixture, close the whipper, insert a charger and make the foam. If you do not have a whipper, emulsify the mixture by whisking it until it becomes frothy.

Arrange the scallops in soup dishes along with the vanilla foam.

Chop up the vanilla pod and use to decorate if desired.

Smoked salmon parcels filled with mussels

Aumônière de moules au saumon fumé

■ **1 serving**
■ **Preparation time**
5 minutes
■ **Cooking time**
5 minutes
■ **Ingredients**
10 cooked mussels
1 teaspoon crème fraîche (3% fat)
(tolerated)
1 large slice of smoked salmon
30g (1oz) fat-free fromage frais
1 chive

Over a gentle heat, warm through the cooked mussels for 5 minutes in a non-stick frying pan. Then, at the last moment, add the low-fat crème fraîche.

Place the slice of smoked salmon on your plate and spread the fromage frais over it. Arrange the mussels on top.

Make the smoked salmon slice into a purse by tying it up with a chive.

Salmon and cucumber millefeuilles

Mille-feuilles de concombre et saumon

- **6 servings**
- **Preparation time**
  15 minutes
- **Ingredients**
  1 cucumber
  175g (6oz) smoked salmon
  50g (1¾oz) fat-free fromage frais
  3 sprigs of thyme
  1 small jar of salmon roe
  Salt and black pepper

Rinse, dry and peel the cucumber. Chop it into 10cm (4 inch) long sections, then cut each piece into thin strips.

Cut the salmon slices in three.

Add a little salt to the cucumber and some black pepper to the smoked salmon. Make up the six individual millefeuilles by alternating two strips of cucumber with one strip of smoked salmon, spreading a little fromage frais between them. Pick off some thyme leaves and scatter on top of each layer. Finish with a slice of cucumber.

Decorate with a sliver of salmon and the salmon roe, then refrigerate until ready to serve.

PHASE 2
PV

Crevettes and cherry tomatoes in a spicy cream

Crevettes sauce curry et ses tomates-cerises

- **2 servings**
- **Preparation time**
  10 minutes
- **Cooking time**
  10 minutes
- **Ingredients**
  16 large prawns (crevettes)
  100ml (3½fl oz) crème fraîche (3% fat) (tolerated)
  15 drops of coconut flavouring (optional)
  www.mydukandietshop.co.uk
  ½ teaspoon curry powder
  ¼ teaspoon mild chilli powder
  8 cherry tomatoes

Peel the prawns, leaving the tails intact, and gently fry them in a non-stick frying pan until golden brown.

In the meantime, make the spicy cream by mixing together the crème fraîche, flavouring, curry powder and chilli powder and heating in a small saucepan.

Pour the sauce into shallow soup bowls and arrange the prawns and cherry tomatoes on top of the cream, adding a couple of cocktail sticks.

Lobster with eggs and smoked salmon

Aspic d'œufs au homard et au saumon fumé

PHASE 2 PV

- **6 servings**
- **Preparation time**
  20 minutes
- **Cooking time**
  30 minutes
- **Refrigeration time**
  2 hours
- **Ingredients**
  3 whole eggs
  1 sachet (25g/1oz) of aspic jelly powder (optional)
  1 bunch of white or green asparagus
  ½ cooked lobster
  3 slices of smoked salmon
  ½ bunch of parsley

Hard-boil the eggs and cut them in half.

Make up the aspic jelly, if using, following the instructions on the sachet.

Peel the asparagus and snap off the woody bottoms of the asparagus spears at their natural breaking point. Cook in salted boiling water for 5 to 10 minutes until the asparagus stalks are tender. Once the asparagus is cooked, drain, place the spears on a clean tea towel to soak up all the water and leave to cool.

Cut up the lobster into medallions and arrange them in a small dish, placing the eggs on top with the yolks facing upwards. Pour over the aspic mixture and refrigerate for at least 2 hours.

When ready to serve, turn the lobster aspic out from the dish and arrange on a big plate or individual ones, with the asparagus arranged around it, along with the smoked salmon slices that have been cut in half. To add a little colour, sprinkle over some chopped parsley.

Baked vegetable terrine

Couronne de légumes grillés

Thinly slice the aubergines and courgettes.

Bake all the vegetables in the oven at 180°C/350°F/Gas 4. As soon as the skin on the peppers starts to blister and turn black, take them out and put them in a plastic bag or in a bowl with a lid so that they can be peeled easily. Once they have cooled, remove the skins and slice.

In a pan, stir the agar-agar into the tomato coulis or stock. Bring to the boil and leave for 2 minutes. Add salt and black pepper.

Take a terrine or savarin mould and in the bottom first arrange the vegetables that will also end up being the decoration on top. Now arrange the remaining vegetables, alternating the red and yellow peppers. Pour in a little of the agar-agar mixture in between the layers and insert a few basil leaves for extra flavour.

Once all the vegetables have been layered, pour in the remaining liquid and press it all down a little. Place a plate or piece of cardboard into the mould, put a heavy weight on top and refrigerate for at least 24 hours.

Just before serving, turn out of the mould and add a little vinaigrette and a few basil leaves for decoration.

- **8 servings**
- **Prepare the day before**
- **Preparation time**
  30 minutes
- **Cooking time**
  25 minutes
- **Refrigeration time**
  24 hours
- **Ingredients**
  2 aubergines
  5 courgettes
  2 red peppers
  2 yellow peppers
  4g agar-agar
  200ml (7fl oz) tomato coulis (see page 154) or 200ml (7fl oz) low-salt chicken stock, with the fat skimmed off (tolerated)
  1 bunch of basil
  A little Dukan vinaigrette (tolerated) (for decoration)
  Salt and black pepper

Salmon and broccoli mousse

PHASE 2
PV

Duo léger saumon-brocoli

- **For 6 or 12 small or shot glasses**
- **Preparation time**
  15 minutes
- **Refrigeration time**
  1 hour
- **Ingredients**
  For the salmon mousse
  150g (5½oz) smoked salmon
  8 tablespoons fat-free fromage frais
  Juice of ½ lemon
  Salt and black pepper
  For the broccoli mousse
  ½ cooked broccoli head
  50g (1¾oz) fat-free fromage frais
  1 tablespoon virtually fat-free quark
  Juice of ½ lemon
  A little curry powder and slices of
  lemon (for decoration)
  Salt and black pepper

Blend the salmon in a food processor with the fromage frais and lemon juice until the mixture is smooth and creamy. Add a little salt and black pepper and pour the mixture into the glasses. Place in the fridge while you prepare the broccoli mousse.

Blend the broccoli with the fromage frais, quark and lemon juice. Add salt and black pepper. Add this mixture to the salmon one. Finish off with a sprinkling of curry powder and refrigerate for 1 hour.

Take the glasses out of the fridge 10 minutes before serving them and decorate with a slice of lemon.

Cucumber appetizers with red roe

Bouchées de concombre aux œufs de lump

PHASE 2
PV

- **4 servings**
- **Preparation time**
  20 minutes
- **Cooking time**
  3 minutes
- **Refrigeration time**
  10 minutes
- **Ingredients**
  ½ top-quality cucumber
  6 tablespoons virtually fat-free quark
  50g (1¾oz) fat-free fromage frais
  1 small jar (100g/3½oz) red
  lumpfish roe

Peel the cucumber with a vegetable peeler, retaining the peel. Place the peel in some boiling water and leave for 3 minutes until it becomes more flexible. Drain and keep at room temperature.

Cut the cucumber into four equal-sized pieces and carefully scoop out the seeds so that you leave a hollow about 1cm (½ inch) deep.

Combine the quark and fromage frais. Fill the cucumber hollows so that there is some mixture piled on top. Finish off with some lumpfish roe.

Cut the cucumber peel lengthways into strips to make little ties to decorate each cucumber appetizer.

Refrigerate for 10 minutes or until ready to serve.

Light leek mousse with a tomato coulis

Mousseline légère aux poireaux, petit jus de tomate

- **4 servings**
- **Preparation time**
  20 minutes
- **Cooking time**
  20 minutes
- **Refrigeration time**
  2 hours
- **Ingredients**
  3 leeks (white part only)
  ½ low-salt stock cube (tolerated)
  400g (14oz) soft tofu
  2 tablespoons teriyaki sauce or
  soy sauce
  2g agar-agar
  150ml (5fl oz) skimmed milk
  Salt and black pepper
  For the tomato coulis
  4 large tomatoes

Wash the leek whites and slice thinly. In a pressure cooker, heat the leeks up with 4 tablespoons water and the half stock cube over a gentle heat. Cover the leeks with water, put the lid on and once the pressure cooker starts to hiss, cook for a further 10 minutes. If you don't have a pressure cooker, cook the leeks in a saucepan with a lid, but you may need to cook for a little longer until soft.

Drain the leeks, then blend them in a food processor with the tofu and teriyaki or soy sauce.

In a pan, combine the agar-agar and skimmed milk (you can also use soya milk). Bring to the boil and simmer for 30 seconds. Add this to the leek mixture and blend it all together. Season with salt and black pepper.

Pour the mixture into four ramekin dishes lined with clingfilm. Leave to cool down to room temperature, then refrigerate for 2 hours.

Poach the tomatoes in boiling water for 30 seconds, then peel them and blend in the food processor with a little water. Pour this tomato coulis onto each plate, turn the leek mousses out of the ramekins and place them carefully on top of the coulis. Decorate according to taste.

Halloween soup

Soupe d'Halloween

- **4 to 6 servings**
- **Preparation time**
  15 minutes
- **Cooking time**
  1 hour
- **Ingredients**
  250g (9oz) pumpkin flesh
  1 medium-sized onion
  1 carrot (tolerated)
  1 fennel bulb
  500ml (18fl oz) skimmed milk
  Salt and black pepper

Remove any seeds and cut the pumpkin flesh into small cubes of about 1cm (½ inch).

Peel and finely chop the onion. Peel and thinly slice the carrot. Cut the fennel bulb into long, thin julienne strips.

In a non-stick frying pan, gently cook the onion, carrot and fennel with 4 tablespoons water. As soon as the water has evaporated, add the little cubes of pumpkin and enough water to cover. Cook with the lid on for 40 minutes, stirring from time to time to make sure that none of the vegetables stick. If they do, just add a little more water to the bottom of the pan.

Heat the milk in a saucepan.

Blend the soup in a food processor, gradually adding the heated milk. Season with salt and black pepper and divide among warmed soup bowls.

Ham mousse with tomato sauce

Verrines de jambon et de tomates en sauce

PHASE 2
PV

- **6 servings**
- **Preparation time**
  20 minutes
- **Refrigeration time**
  1 hour
- **Ingredients**
  For the ham mousse
  100g (3½oz) extra-lean ham (or
  cooked turkey or chicken)
  30g (1oz) fat-free fromage frais
  100ml (3½fl oz) crème fraîche (3%
  fat) (tolerated)
  1 pinch of paprika
  Black pepper
  For the tomato sauce
  200g (7oz) chopped tomatoes
  1 garlic clove
  50g (1¾oz) fat-free fromage frais
  1 teaspoon chopped chives
  A few basil leaves, chopped chives,
  pieces of ham and paprika (for
  decoration)

Blend the ingredients for the mousse and the sauce separately in a food processor so that you end up with two mixtures.

Leave them to rest for about an hour in the fridge.

Then make up the concoctions in a glass, starting with the layer of tomato sauce followed by the layer of ham mousse.

Decorate with one or two basil leaves, the chives, ham and a sprinkling of paprika.

Summer seafood surprise

Verrines fraîcheur

- **6 servings**
- **Preparation time**
  15 minutes
- **Ingredients**
  3 tablespoons grated seafood sticks
  (surimi)
  ½ cooked broccoli head
  Juice of 1 lime
  50g (1¾oz) fat-free fromage frais
  2 tablespoons crème fraîche (3% fat)
  (tolerated)
  1 teaspoon dill, finely chopped
  3 slices of smoked salmon
  A few chopped chives and dill (for
  decoration)
  Black pepper

Put a little of the grated seafood sticks into each glass.

Purée the ½ broccoli head in a food processor and sprinkle the lime juice over it. Spread a layer of this purée over the seafood sticks.

Blend the fromage frais with the crème fraîche, finely chopped dill and add black pepper. Add a layer of this mixture on top of the broccoli.

Cut up the smoked salmon into strips, roll them up and place on top of the fromage frais mixture.

Decorate with a little of the grated seafood sticks and some chives and dill.

Smoked salmon and cucumber jellies

Concombre au cœur de saumon fumé

- **6 servings**
- **Preparation time**
  30 minutes
- **Refrigeration time**
  6 hours
- **Ingredients**
  1 cucumber
  1 teaspoon agar-agar
  2 large slices of smoked salmon
  1 pinch of salt

Boil 250ml (9fl oz) water with a pinch of salt.

In the meantime, peel the cucumber and remove the seeds.

As soon as the water comes to the boil, add the agar-agar, stirring it in well so that it all dissolves, and let this boil for 2 minutes. Remove from the heat, put the cucumber in the water and then blend it all in a food processor.

Cut up the smoked salmon into thin shavings.

Arrange the salmon in six small silicone or dariole moulds to cover the bottom, then fill up the moulds with the blended cucumber mix. Leave to cool so that the mixture sets.

Refrigerate for at least 6 hours before serving.

Sweet pepper soup with ginger

Soupe de poivrons au gingembre

- **4 servings**
- **Preparation time**
  20 minutes
- **Cooking time**
  50 minutes
- **Ingredients**
  3 red peppers
  1 red onion
  2 garlic cloves
  1 piece (5cm/2 inch) of fresh ginger, grated
  1 teaspoon ground cumin
  1 teaspoon ground coriander
  1 tablespoon cornflour (tolerated)
  900ml (1½ pints) low-salt chicken stock, with the fat skimmed off (tolerated)
  4 tablespoons fat-free fromage frais (to decorate)
  Salt and black pepper

Preheat the oven to 200°C/400°F/Gas 6.

Cut the peppers in half, peel and quarter the onion and place on a non-stick baking tray along with the unpeeled garlic cloves. As soon as the skin on the peppers starts to blister and turn black, take them out and put them in a plastic bag or in a bowl with a lid so that they can be peeled easily. Once they have cooled, remove the skins.

In a non-stick frying pan, heat 4 tablespoons water and gently cook the ginger, cumin and coriander for 5 minutes. Add the cornflour, stirring it in thoroughly, and season. Pour in the chicken stock, cover and simmer for 30 minutes.

Peel and crush the garlic cloves. Add the onion and garlic to the soup.

Keep one pepper half back to cut into thin strips, and add the others to the soup mixture. Simmer for a further 5 minutes.

Blend the soup in a food processor until it has a smooth texture, pour it into a saucepan and heat it through.

When ready to serve, add a tablespoonful of fat-free fromage frais, if desired, and some strips of pepper to decorate each bowl.

Summer cocktail topped with bresaola

Cocktail fraîcheur de viande des Grisons

■ **6 servings**
■ **Preparation time**
   20 minutes
■ **Ingredients**
   3 medium-sized tomatoes
   6 carrots (tolerated)
   300g (10½oz) celery sticks
   A handful of chervil or parsley
   6 pinches of curry powder
   6-12 slices of bresaola
   Salt and black pepper

Poach the tomatoes in boiling water for 30 seconds, then peel and deseed them. Peel, wash and chop the carrots. Remove any leaves from the celery and slice into sticks.

Blend all the vegetables in a food processor and add salt and black pepper.

Pour this mixture into six glasses, then sprinkle over a pinch of curry powder and add the chervil. Finally, roll up the bresaola slices and add one or two to each glass.

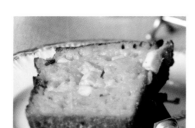

Pumpkin loaf

Cake au potiron

- **8 servings**
- **Preparation time**
  15 minutes
- **Cooking time**
  1 hour 5 minutes
- **Ingredients**
  1 pumpkin (to get 400g/14oz
  pumpkin flesh)
  3 eggs
  10 drops of melted butter flavouring
  (optional)
  www.mydukandietshop.co.uk
  100ml (3½fl oz) skimmed milk
  50g (1¾oz) wholemeal flour
  50g (1¾oz) oat bran
  1 teaspoon baking powder
  150g (5½oz) cooked chicken,
  chopped into small sticks
  100g (3½oz) Emmental or other hard
  cheese (5% fat), grated
  A little parsley
  A little nutmeg
  Salt and black pepper

Remove the pumpkin skin and cut 400g (14oz) of the pumpkin flesh into cubes of about 1cm (½ inch). Cook them in a non-stick frying pan with 4 tablespoons water. Keep stirring from time to time and add more water whenever necessary.

After about 15 minutes, use the tip of a knife to check whether they are cooked and once the knife goes in easily, remove the pan from the heat. Purée in a blender and then put to one side.

Preheat the oven to 220°C/425°F/Gas 7.

In a bowl, whisk the eggs with the butter flavouring to produce an omelette mixture. Add the pumpkin purée, milk, flour, oat bran and baking powder. Stir together well. Fold in the chicken bits and Emmental. Add some parsley, nutmeg, salt and black pepper.

Pour the mixture into a loaf tin or a soufflé mould and bake in the oven for 50 minutes. Check to see if the loaf is cooked by inserting a knife and it should come out clean.

Main courses

Spicy omelette with fresh mint

Omelette à la menthe et au curry

PHASE 1/ PHASE 2 PP

- **2 servings**
- **Preparation time**
  5 minutes
- **Cooking time**
  10 minutes
- **Ingredients**
  4 eggs
  50g (1¾oz) fat-free fromage frais
  1 generous pinch of curry powder
  A few fresh mint leaves
  Salt and black pepper

In a bowl, beat together the eggs and fromage frais. Add salt, black pepper and the curry powder.

Chop up the mint leaves and add them to the mixture. Stir them in well.

In a non-stick frying pan, pour in half the mixture and cook both sides of the omelette over a gentle heat, then slide out on to a plate to serve.

Repeat with the remaining mixture to make the second omelette.

Medallions of sole with salmon

Médaillons de sole au saumon

- ■ **4 servings**
- ■ **Preparation time**
  20 minutes
- ■ **Cooking time**
  20 minutes
- ■ **Ingredients**
  160g (5½oz) salmon steak
  4 fillets of sole
  1 lemon
  Sea salt and black pepper

Preheat the oven to 200°C/400°F/Gas 6.

Cut the salmon steak into four pieces, removing any skin.

Prepare the four fillets of sole, removing any bones or pieces of skin.

Take each fillet, place a piece of salmon on top and roll the fillet of sole around it. Tie each one together with a piece of kitchen string.

Place the medallions in an ovenproof dish. Sprinkle a little sea salt and freshly ground black pepper over them and drizzle some lemon juice on top.

Bake for 20 minutes.

In the Cruise phase (PV), serve with a tomato coulis (see page 154).

PHASE 2
PV

Seafood sauerkraut

Choucroute aux fruits de mer

- **4 servings**
- **Preparation time**
  30 minutes
- **Cooking time**
  1 hour 15 minutes
- **Ingredients**
  2kg (4½lb) sauerkraut, uncooked
  10 juniper berries
  100ml (3½fl oz) Riesling (tolerated)
  600g (1¼lb) ling or cod fillets
  12 scallops
  6 mussels
  2 smoked haddock fillets
  6 prawns, shell on
  6 thin slices of smoked eel (optional)
  Some dill (for decoration)
  Salt and black pepper
  Wooden kebab sticks, 12cm
  (5 inches) long

  For the sauce
  2 shallots
  100ml (3½fl oz) Riesling (tolerated)
  10 drops of melted butter flavouring
  (optional)
  www.mydukandietshop.co.uk
  Salt and black pepper

Rinse the raw sauerkraut several times and put in a pressure cooker basket along with the juniper berries. Sprinkle over the Riesling, add 400ml (14fl oz) water and cook for 1 hour 15 minutes. If you cannot find uncooked sauerkraut, you can use cooked sauerkraut from a jar or packet. The sauerkraut just needs to be heated and the fish and seafood can be cooked in the pressure cooker or a steamer.

Cut the fish fillets into 16 cubes and sprinkle black pepper over them. Using the wooden kebab sticks, make up kebabs by alternating the fish cubes with the scallops.

Scrub the mussels and rinse well, discarding any that are broken or don't close.

Twenty minutes before the sauerkraut has finished cooking, add the kebabs to the basket of the pressure cooker or steamer. Ten minutes later, add the smoked haddock and mussels, then 7 minutes afterwards, place the prawns and sliced eel in the basket too.

Whilst the sauerkraut is cooking, prepare the sauce. Finely chop the shallots and put them in a pan with the wine, butter flavouring and 5 tablespoons water. Add salt and black pepper. Reduce over a high heat until thickened. Keep the sauce warm in a *bain-marie* until ready to serve.

Arrange the sauerkraut on a heated serving dish and place the fish and seafood on top, discarding any mussels that haven't opened. Decorate with a few sprigs of dill and serve the sauce separately.

Salt cod gratin with chanterelle mushrooms

PHASE 2
PV

Gratin de morue aux girolles

- **4 servings**
  Soak the salt cod the day before
- **Preparation time**
  30 minutes
- **Cooking time**
  40 minutes
- **Ingredients**
  600g (1¼lb) salt cod
  1 small bunch of thyme
  2 onions
  4 cloves
  2 bay leaves
  1 bunch of parsley
  400ml (14fl oz) low-salt chicken
  stock, with the fat skimmed off
  (tolerated)
  250g (9oz) chanterelle mushrooms
  3 garlic cloves
  200ml (7fl oz) crème fraîche (3% fat)
  (tolerated)
  2 handfuls of Emmental or other hard
  cheese (5% fat), grated
  Salt and black pepper

The day before, soak the fish, skin up, to get rid of the salt.

Heat some water in a casserole dish and place the fish in it along with the thyme, one of the onions studded with the 4 cloves, the bay leaf and a little parsley. Cook for 10 minutes.

Pour 200ml (7fl oz) of the chicken stock into a frying pan. Add the chanterelle mushrooms, having washed them beforehand, season with salt and black pepper and cook until tender.

Take the salt cod out of the casserole dish and remove the skin and any bones.

Preheat the oven to 180°C/350°F/Gas 4.

Put the crushed garlic and chopped parsley in with the cooked mushrooms. Stir, turn off the heat, cover the pan with a lid, then leave the chanterelle mushrooms to soak up the flavours while you cook the other onion.

In a non-stick frying pan, gently cook the other finely chopped onion until softened, then pour in the remaining 200ml (7fl oz) stock. Leave to simmer away over a gentle heat until all the water has evaporated.

Heat the frying pan again with the chanterelle mushrooms, add the onion and flaked cod, stir, and then work in the crème fraîche. Pour this mixture into a gratin dish, scatter over the Emmental and bake in the oven for 20 minutes.

Mediterranean cockles

Coques méditerranéennes

- **2 to 4 servings**
- **Preparation time**
  10 minutes
- **Cooking time**
  35 minutes
- **Ingredients**
  6 shallots
  400g (14oz) tin of chopped tomatoes
  1 teaspoon Brandy (Cognac)
  flavouring (optional)
  www.mydukandietshop.co.uk
  1 sprig of thyme
  1 tablespoon fresh or 1 teaspoon
  dried oregano
  100ml (3½fl oz) crème fraîche (3%
  fat) (tolerated)
  1 tablespoon cornflour (tolerated)
  1kg (2¼lb) cockles

Finely chop the shallots and gently cook in 4 tablespoons water until softened. Turn up the heat and add the tomatoes, flavouring, herbs, crème fraîche and the cornflour diluted in 2 tablespoons water. Reduce for about 5 minutes.

Add the cockles, having washed them beforehand, and cook everything over a medium heat for 25 minutes.

Serve with the vegetables of your choice.

Rabbit with a mustard sauce and braised chicory

Lapin à la moutarde et ses endives braisées

- **4 servings**
- **Preparation time**
  15 minutes
- **Cooking time**
  55 minutes
- **Ingredients**
  1 teaspoon oil (tolerated)
  1 rabbit, cut into pieces (you could also use chicken)
  2 shallots
  500ml (18fl oz) low-salt stock, with the fat skimmed off (tolerated)
  3 tablespoons mustard (Dijon or wholegrain) (tolerated)
  2 tablespoons crème fraîche (3% fat) (tolerated)
  1 good pinch of ground ginger
  1 tablespoon chopped parsley and garlic
  2 sprigs of rosemary
  Salt and black pepper
  For the chicory
  300g (10½oz) chicory
  1 low-salt stock cube (tolerated)
  1 tablespoon chopped parsley and garlic
  Black pepper

Using a kitchen towel, oil the bottom of a large casserole dish. Place the rabbit pieces in the casserole and sear them on all sides until they start to brown. Add the peeled and finely chopped shallots, stirring until they turn golden brown. Pour in 100ml (3½fl oz) water, the stock, add some black pepper, cover and leave to simmer for 30 minutes.

Next add the mustard, crème fraîche, ginger, chopped parsley and garlic and rosemary. Stir well, using a wooden spoon. Cook for a further 15 minutes.

Whilst the rabbit is simmering away, prepare the chicory. Cut the chicory into slices of about 2cm (¾ inch), wash and place on a clean tea towel to absorb the water. Then put the chicory slices in a frying pan and let them cook gently until soft. Crumble in the stock cube and add 100ml (3½fl oz) water. Season with a little black pepper and finish off with some chopped parsley and garlic. Leave to simmer until all the water has evaporated.

Serve the rabbit and mustard sauce with a spoonful of the braised chicory.

Asian-style mussels

Moules à l'orientale

PHASE 2
PV

- **2 servings**
- **Preparation time**
  10 minutes
- **Cooking time**
  10 minutes
- **Ingredients**
  1kg (2¼lb) mussels
  140g (5oz) tin of tomato purée
  2 shallots
  1 teaspoon ground cumin
  1 pinch of ground ginger
  ½ bunch of parsley

Scrub the mussels and rinse well, discarding any that are broken or open.

Cover the mussels halfway with water in a large pan and pour in the tomato purée.

Peel, then finely chop the shallots and add to the mussels. Add the cumin, ginger and a little chopped parsley and cook over a high heat for 3 to 7 minutes until they open up (discard any that have not opened).

As soon as the mussels open up, they are ready to serve.

Aniseed-flavoured veal stew with fennel

Blanquette de veau anisée au fenouil

- **4 servings**
- **Preparation time**
  35 minutes
- **Cooking time**
  1 hour 15 minutes
- **Ingredients**
  4 fennel bulbs
  1 large onion
  4 carrots (tolerated)
  1 leek
  800g (1¾lb) veal, trimmed of any fat
  1 low-salt stock cube (tolerated)
  2 cloves
  2 star anise
  2 bay leaves
  2 tablespoons cornflour (tolerated)
  800g (1¾lb) butternut squash
  1 teaspoon curry powder
  Salt and black pepper

Remove the hard root end at the base of each fennel bulb.

Peel and finely chop the onion. Peel and thinly slice the carrots. Cut the fennel and leek into thin slices. Place the vegetables in a colander and wash them. Chop up the meat into big chunks.

In a non-stick frying pan, gently cook the meat and onion. As soon as the meat starts to turn brown, cover it with water and crumble in the stock cube. Stir thoroughly. Add the vegetables, cloves, star anise and bay leaves. Season with salt and black pepper and bring to the boil. Stir, then leave to simmer over a gentle heat for 1 hour. At the last moment, stir in the cornflour. Taste and, if necessary, adjust the seasoning.

In the meantime, remove the skin from the butternut squash and cut into 1cm (½ inch) cubes. Cook them in a non-stick frying pan with a little water in the bottom for 30 to 40 minutes. Add more water whenever necessary. When cooked, add the curry powder and season with salt and black pepper. Use a fork to mash the squash a little.

Serve the stew on warmed plates along with the butternut squash purée.

In the Consolidation phase, you could serve this stew with brown rice or couscous.

PHASE 2
PV

Carrot flan

Flan à la carotte

- **4 servings**
- **Preparation time**
  15 minutes
- **Cooking time**
  20 minutes
- **Ingredients**
  200g (7oz) carrots (tolerated)
  2 eggs
  200g (7oz) fat-free fromage frais or
  100g (3½oz) fat-free fromage frais +
  100ml (3½fl oz) crème fraîche (3%
  fat) (tolerated)
  ¼ teaspoon ground nutmeg
  1 generous handful of Emmental or
  other hard cheese (5% fat), grated
  (tolerated)
  1 teaspoon oil (tolerated)
  A little parsley
  Salt and black pepper

Preheat the oven to 240°C/475°F/Gas 9.

Peel, wash and grate the carrots.

In a large bowl, whisk together the eggs, fromage frais, nutmeg and Emmental. Add salt and black pepper (you can also substitute different spices and use curry powder, cumin etc.)

Using some kitchen paper, oil four ramekins (or one large ovenproof flan dish) and divide the grated carrots among them. Scatter over a little parsley, then pour the creamy egg mixture on top.

Place the ramekins or flan dish on a baking tray and bake in the oven for 20 minutes.

Leave to cool down a little, then turn the flans out onto plates and sprinkle over a little more parsley if desired. You may need a knife to turn them out.

This carrot flan is an excellent accompaniment for white meat.

PHASE 2
PV

Mushroom and tofu quiche

Quiche aux champignons et au tofu soyeux

- **8 servings**
- **Preparation time**
  20 minutes
- **Cooking time**
  45 minutes
- **Ingredients**
  600g (1¼lb) mushrooms (a mixture of button, field and oyster mushrooms)
  A little parsley
  400g (14oz) soft tofu
  4 eggs
  2 handfuls of Emmental or other hard cheese (5% fat), grated (tolerated)
  ½ teaspoon ground nutmeg
  8 cherry tomatoes
  Salt and black pepper

Preheat the oven to 240°C/475°F/Gas 9.

Wash the mushrooms under a slow tap or just wipe clean, then dry with a clean tea towel. Slice thinly and gently fry them in a non-stick frying pan with some parsley. Add salt and black pepper.

In the meantime, mix together the tofu, eggs, Emmental and nutmeg in a bowl. As soon as the mushrooms start to turn golden brown, add them in too. Stir everything together thoroughly and adjust the seasoning if necessary.

Pour the mixture into an ovenproof dish and arrange the cherry tomatoes, pushing them in slightly. Scatter a little parsley on top if desired.

Bake in the oven for 40 minutes. Check the quiche and leave a little longer if not completely cooked.

This quiche goes well with a nice salad.

Squashes filled with veal Bolognese

Potimarron et bolognaise de veau

PHASE 2
PV

- **4 servings**
- **Preparation time**
  15 minutes
- **Cooking time**
  50 minutes
- **Ingredients**
  2 Hokkaido squashes (potimarrons)
  1 onion
  400g (14oz) minced veal
  250g (9oz) passata
  ½ teaspoon mild chilli powder
  1 generous pinch of ground ginger
  A little parsley
  Salt and black pepper

Preheat the oven to 240°C/475°F/Gas 9.

Cut both squashes lengthways and, using a spoon, scoop out the seeds. Put the squash halves in the oven for 20 minutes.

In the meantime, peel and finely chop the onion and mix it in with the minced veal. Gently fry in a non-stick frying pan and, as soon as all the meat is browned, add the passata, spices and parsley. Season with salt and black pepper.

Once the squash halves are cooked through, take them out of the oven and fill them with the veal bolognese.

Bake in the oven for 30 minutes.

Curried chicken club sandwich

Suprêmes cheeseburger au curry

- **2 servings**
- **Preparation time**
  15 minutes
- **Cooking time**
  15 minutes
- **Ingredients**
  1 large onion
  ½ teaspoon curry powder
  1 large tomato
  A few lettuce leaves
  Some extra-light cream cheese (4 to 6% fat) (in the Cruise phase) or 4 slices of low-fat Cheddar (in the Consolidation phase)
  2 slices of cooked chicken
  A little reduced sugar and salt ketchup
  For the Dukan sandwich bread
  3 generous tablespoons oat bran
  1 teaspoon baking powder
  2 tablespoons fat-free fromage frais
  1 egg + 2 egg whites

In a bowl, combine all the bread ingredients in the following order: the bran, baking powder, fromage frais and eggs. Pour this mixture into two small round moulds. Microwave for 5 minutes and leave to cool.

Peel and thinly slice the onion. In a frying pan, cook in a little water with the curry powder.

Wash and slice the tomato. Wash the lettuce leaves.

As soon as the bread circles have cooled, remove them from the moulds, slice them in two and toast them on the highest setting.

Put two of the bread halves on a plate. On each of them, add a little of the ketchup, then stack up some curry-flavoured onion slices, sliced tomato and lettuce leaves. Add some sliced cooked chicken on the top half with the cheese. Place the other bread halves on top and enjoy…

In the Attack and Cruise phases, remember you should not eat more than 2 tablespoonfuls of oat bran per day.

Chilli con carne with tofu

Chili con carne au tofu

- **2 servings**
- **Preparation time**
  10 minutes
- **Cooking time**
  25 minutes
- **Ingredients**
  2 garlic cloves
  2 onions
  300g (10½oz) firm tofu
  2 green chillies
  400g (14oz) minced beef
  500g (1lb 2oz) passata
  1 tablespoon chilli powder
  1 bay leaf
  ¼ teaspoon ground cumin
  Salt and black pepper

Chop the garlic, cut the onions into small pieces, crumble the tofu and dice the green chillies, then place these with the beef in a non-stick frying pan and gently fry for 5 minutes. Add all the other ingredients and mix together thoroughly. Season with salt and black pepper.

As soon as the ingredients come to the boil, cover, turn the heat down slightly and leave to simmer for 15 minutes.

Depending on your own preferences, this dish could be served with some steamed courgettes or a nice salad.

Aubergine and tofu lasagne

Lasagnes d'aubergine au tofu

PHASE 2
PV

- **2 servings**
- **Preparation time**
  25 minutes
- **Resting time**
  30 minutes
- **Cooking time**
  35 minutes
- **Ingredients**
  1 medium-sized aubergine
  1 courgette
  1 or 2 tomatoes
  100g (3½oz) firm tofu (herb-flavoured if you can find it)
  1 onion
  1 garlic clove
  ½ low-salt chicken stock cube (tolerated)
  1 teaspoon Italian herb seasoning
  A little Emmental or other hard cheese (5% fat), grated (tolerated)
  Salt

Cut the aubergine into thin slices, sprinkle it with salt and leave to drain for at least 30 minutes. Rinse the aubergine slices in cold water and wipe dry.

Preheat the oven to 240°C/475°F/Gas 9.

Thinly slice the courgette and tomatoes. Cut the tofu into thin slices and then finely chop the onion and garlic.

In a non-stick frying pan, cook the aubergine slices in 4 tablespoons water with the crumbled half stock cube for a few minutes until they turn slightly brown.

Do the same with the courgette slices and tofu in separate pans. Put to one side.

Gently cook the onion and garlic for 1 or 2 minutes in 2 tablespoons water and add the tomato. Sprinkle over the Italian herb seasoning.

In an ovenproof dish, arrange the aubergine slices so that they completely cover the bottom. Place the courgettes on top of the aubergines. Make another layer with the tofu slices and scatter a little low-fat grated Emmental on top. Add the tomato, onion and garlic. Bake in the oven for 25 minutes.

Five minutes before the lasagne is ready to come out of the oven, sprinkle some more grated Emmental over the top.

PHASE 2
PV

Stir-fried beef with sweet peppers

Bœuf aux poivrons

- **2 servings**
- **Preparation time**
  15 minutes
- **Cooking time**
  20 minutes
- **Ingredients**
  2 red peppers
  1 green pepper
  400g (14oz) rump steak
  2 shallots
  1 teaspoon soy sauce
  Some herbes de Provence (mixed herbs)
  Salt and black pepper

Halve and deseed the peppers, then thinly slice them. Cut the meat into cubes.

In a large non-stick frying pan, gently fry the finely chopped shallots and cubes of meat for 5 to 10 minutes. Season with salt.

Add the thin slices of pepper and cook for a further 10 minutes, stirring all the time.

Two minutes before you are ready to serve, pour in the soy sauce.

Season with salt and black pepper and scatter over the herbs.

Red mullet fillets with basil

Filets de rouget au basilic

- **3 servings**
- **Preparation time**
  15 minutes
- **Cooking time**
  10 minutes
- **Ingredients**
  350g (12oz) tomatoes
  1 garlic clove
  1 bunch of basil
  2 teaspoons olive oil (tolerated)
  6 red mullet fillets
  1 tablespoon balsamic vinegar
  (tolerated)
  Salt and black pepper

Wash the tomatoes and chop them up into small, even pieces. Peel the garlic. Wash and dry the basil and remove the leaves from the stems.

Mince the basil roughly in a blender, adding the garlic and 1 teaspoon of the olive oil.

Wipe the red mullet fillets dry with some kitchen paper. Using a pastry brush, brush them all over with the rest of the olive oil. Warm a non-stick frying pan and fry the fillets for 2 minutes on each side over a high heat. Season with salt. Remove the fillets from the pan and keep them warm.

Pour the vinegar into the frying pan and use a spatula to scrape the pan and dissolve the cooking juices. Simmer for 1 minute. Add the tomatoes. Heat them for 2 minutes in the cooking juices in the pan, stirring well so that the tomatoes get completely covered with the juices. Purée the sauce in a blender and add salt and black pepper.

Transfer the tomatoes onto a large serving dish. Arrange the red mullet fillets on top of this bed of tomatoes. Top with the basil purée (you could also decorate them with some nice sprigs of basil). Serve straightaway.

Chicken, apple and vegetable curry

Poulet au curry et ses légumes

PHASE 3

- **2 servings**
- **Preparation time**
  20 minutes
- **Cooking time**
  1 hour
- **Ingredients**
  1 aubergine
  2 courgettes
  2 onions
  1 teaspoon olive oil (tolerated)
  1 low-salt chicken stock cube
  (tolerated)
  2 teaspoons curry powder
  1 tablespoon chopped parsley and
  garlic
  2 chicken breasts
  1 apple
  1 pinch of ginger
  100ml (3½fl oz) crème fraîche
  (3% fat) (tolerated)
  Salt and black pepper

Wash and dice the aubergine and courgettes. Peel and finely chop one onion.

Fry the vegetables for 10 minutes in a non-stick frying pan with the olive oil and 4 tablespoons water. If the vegetables start to stick, add a little more water.

Crumble in one half of the stock cube and add enough water to cover. Combine thoroughly and add 1 teaspoon curry powder along with the chopped parsley and garlic. Season with salt and black pepper. Leave to simmer for 20 minutes over a gentle heat, adding a little more water if necessary.

Cut the chicken breasts into pieces. Peel and finely chop the remaining onion. Peel the apple and slice it thinly.

Cook the onion and apple in a non-stick frying pan with 4 tablespoons water. As soon as they have softened, crumble in the other half of the stock cube and add 4 tablespoons water. Add the chicken pieces and let them cook through, then stir in the remaining curry powder and ginger and leave to simmer for about 10 minutes. Season with a little salt and black pepper.

Just before serving, mix the vegetables and chicken together and add the crème fraîche.

Normandy-style coquilles Saint-Jacques

Coquilles Saint-Jacques normandes

- **2 servings**
- **Preparation time**
  20 minutes
- **Cooking time**
  20 minutes
- **Ingredients**
  4 teaspoons mustard (tolerated)
  1 small bunch of fresh herbs, finely chopped
  300g (10½oz) tomatoes
  1 large apple
  300g (10½oz) scallops
  2 shallots
  1 good pinch of paprika
  1 lemon
  2 tablespoons crème fraîche (3% fat) (tolerated)
  A little parsley, chopped
  Salt and black pepper

Preheat the oven to 180°C/350°F/Gas 4.

Mix together the mustard and fresh herbs with some salt and black pepper.

Cut a thin lid off the top of the tomatoes and place the tomatoes in a gratin dish. Divide the herb mixture among the tomatoes, put their lids back on and bake in the oven for 20 minutes.

In the meantime, peel and slice the apple.

In a non-stick frying pan, gently fry the scallops with the sliced apple until lightly browned. Add the finely chopped shallots and season with a little salt, black pepper and paprika. Next stir in some lemon juice and crème fraîche. Reduce a little over a very gentle heat.

Arrange the scallops on warmed plates, scatter over a little chopped parsley and serve with the baked tomatoes.

Coconut chicken with French beans and tofu

Poulet au lait de coco et ses haricots au tofu

- **2 servings**
- **Preparation time**
  10 minutes
- **Cooking time**
  15 minutes
- **Ingredients**
  2 chicken breasts
  200ml (7fl oz) coconut milk
  1 teaspoon curry powder
  100-150g (3½-5½oz) firm tofu
  2 handfuls of French beans
  A few long chives
  A few sesame and poppy seeds
  Salt and black pepper

Cut the chicken breasts into cubes and cook in a non-stick frying pan until just browned. Add the coconut milk and curry powder, and simmer until cooked through.

Dice up the tofu, and gently fry the tofu cubes in a separate frying pan until lightly browned. Add some salt, black pepper, and two tablespoons of the coconut sauce from the chicken pan, and cook for a further 2 minutes.

Meanwhile, top and tail the French beans and cook in salted boiling water until tender. When just cool enough to handle, tie the beans up into two bundles using lengths of chive.

Arrange the chicken on plates with the curry coconut milk sauce, then add the tofu cubes.

Serve with the French bean bundles and, as a finishing touch, sprinkle a few sesame and poppy seeds over the tofu cubes.

Chicken and prawns in a spicy coconut sauce

Crevettes et poulet sauce coco aux épices

- **2 servings**
- **Preparation time**
  20 minutes
- **Cooking time**
  20 minutes
- **Ingredients**
  1 chicken breast
  300g (10½oz) prawns, peeled but tails left on
  2 garlic cloves
  1 onion
  1 teaspoon curry powder
  ½ teaspoon mild chilli powder
  200ml (7fl oz) coconut milk
  6 white or green asparagus spears, cooked or from a jar
  Salt and black pepper

Cut the chicken breast into pieces and fry over a gentle heat in a non-stick frying pan with a little water in the bottom of the pan. As soon as the water has evaporated, add the peeled prawns. Cook over a gentle heat for 1 minute, stirring all the time with a wooden spoon.

Peel the garlic and onion. Put them through a small food processor.

Put 4 tablespoons water in another frying pan and add the garlic/onion mixture. Heat it gently for 1 minute and add the spices. Season with a little salt and black pepper. Lastly, pour in the coconut milk and leave to simmer for 5 minutes, stirring occasionally.

Add the prawns and chicken pieces and combine. Cook for 5 minutes over a gentle heat.

Heat up the cooked asparagus either for 5 minutes in a frying pan or microwave them for 1 minute.

Arrange the asparagus on the plates and add the chicken and prawn mixture in the spicy coconut sauce.

Desserts

Muesli ice cream

Glace au muesli

PHASE 1/
PHASE 2
PP

- **2 servings**
- **Preparation time**
  15 minutes
- **Cooking time**
  15 minutes
- **Freezing and cooling time**
  4½ hours
- **Ingredients**
  ½ vanilla pod
  250ml (9fl oz) skimmed milk
  4 tablespoons oat bran
  3 tablespoons sweetener (or more according to taste)
  1 egg
  30g (1oz) fat-free fromage frais
  30g (1oz) virtually fat-free quark
  20 drops of Grand Marnier flavouring (optional), orange flower water or some orange zest
  www.mydukandietshop.co.uk

Split the half vanilla pod, scrape out the seeds and place in a pan with the milk. Bring the milk to the boil. Remove from the heat and add the oat bran and 1 tablespoon of the powdered sweetener. Carefully combine, then place the pan back over a low heat and allow the bran mixture to thicken. Stir in the beaten egg, then remove the pan from the heat and take out the vanilla pod.

In a large bowl, mix together the fromage frais, quark, remaining sweetener and flavouring. Stir in the bran mixture.

Next, pour the mixture into glass dishes and leave for 30 minutes to cool down to room temperature.

Once cooled down, put the glasses in the freezer for at least 4 hours. Give the mixture a stir every hour to prevent crystals forming.

In the Attack and Cruise phases, remember you should not eat more than 2 tablespoonfuls of oat bran per day.

PHASE 1/
PHASE 2
PP

Fluffy pistachio mousses

Mousse aérienne à la pistache

- **8 to 10 servings**
- **Preparation time**
  15 minutes
- **Cooking time**
  5 minutes
- **Refrigeration time**
  4 hours
- **Ingredients**
  3 gelatine leaves
  2-3 tablespoons sweetener
  (according to taste)
  2 teaspoons pistachio flavouring
  (optional)
  www.mydukandietshop.co.uk
  or peppermint flavouring (for mint
  mousses)
  5 drops of green food colouring
  (optional)
  4 egg whites
  1 pinch of salt
  400g (14oz) fat-free fromage frais

Leave the gelatine leaves to soak for 5 minutes in cold water.

Put the sweetener in a saucepan and add 4 tablespoons water. Bring to the boil and leave to boil for 2 minutes. Next add the pistachio flavouring, drained gelatine leaves and food colouring. Stir together well and remove from the heat.

In a bowl, whisk the egg whites with a pinch of salt until stiff. Slowly trickle in the flavoured syrup, whisking all the time. Gently fold the egg whites into the fromage frais, taking care not to break the eggs up.

Divide up the mixture among eight to ten small glasses and refrigerate for 4 hours before serving.

Iced chocolate soufflés

Soufflé glacé au chocolat

- **8 servings**
- **Preparation time**
  15 minutes
- **Cooking time**
  5 minutes
- **Freezing time**
  8 hours
- **Ingredients**
  3 gelatine leaves
  8 tablespoons reduced-fat cocoa
  powder (tolerated)
  1 teaspoon mocha coffee flavouring
  (optional) or very strong coffee
  www.mydukandietshop.co.uk
  2 eggs
  1 pinch of salt
  10 tablespoons fat-free fromage frais
  4 tablespoons sweetener

Leave the gelatine leaves to soak for 5 minutes in cold water.

In a saucepan, gently warm the cocoa powder with 100ml (3½fl oz) water and the coffee flavouring. Remove from the heat and add 2 egg yolks and the softened gelatine.

In a bowl, whisk the egg whites with a pinch of salt until stiff.

Use a whisk to blend together the fromage frais and sweetener, and then add the cocoa mixture. Stir together thoroughly and gently fold in the whisked egg whites. Pour this mixture into eight glasses, moulds or ramekins, then put them in the freezer for 8 hours.

Take the soufflés out of the freezer 10 minutes before you are ready to serve.

Tofu choc cream
Crème tofuchoc

PHASE 2
PP

- **6 to 8 servings**
- **Preparation time**
  5 minutes
- **Refrigeration time**
  1 hour
- **Ingredients**
  200g (7oz) soft tofu
  4 tablespoons fat-free fromage frais
  300g (10½oz) fat-free vanilla yoghurt
  2 teaspoons reduced-fat cocoa
  powder (tolerated)
  2 tablespoons sweetener (or more
  according to taste)

Blend together the tofu, fromage frais, yoghurt, reduced-fat cocoa and sweetener until the mixture is nice and creamy.

Pour the mixture into glasses and refrigerate for 1 hour.

St Tropez tart
La tropézienne

PHASE 2
PP

- **6 servings**
- **Preparation time**
  25 minutes
- **Cooking and cooling time**
  2 hours
- **Ingredients**
  3 tablespoons oat bran
  1 tablespoon cornflour (tolerated)
  1 tablespoon skimmed milk powder
  2 eggs
  150g (5½oz) fat-free natural yoghurt
  15g (½oz) virtually fat-free quark
  15g (½oz) fat-free fromage frais
  1 teaspoon baking powder
  2 tablespoons sweetener
  1½ teaspoons orange flower water

  For the filling
  2 gelatine leaves
  1 vanilla pod
  500ml (18fl oz) skimmed milk
  3 eggs
  2 tablespoons sweetener
  2 tablespoons cornflour (tolerated)
  1 tablespoon white rum flavouring
  (optional)
  www.mydukandietshop.co.uk
  1 sachet (6g) powdered gelatine
  1 pinch of salt

Preheat the oven to 180°C/350°F/Gas 4.

Combine all the brioche ingredients and pour into a silicone mould. Bake in the oven for 20 minutes. Leave to cool, then cut the cake into two layers.

Leave the gelatine leaves to soak for 5 minutes in cold water.

Split the vanilla pod, scrape out the seeds and place in a pan with the milk. Bring the milk to the boil.

In the meantime, mix together the egg yolks, sweetener, cornflour and flavouring in a bowl. Keep the egg whites for later.

Remove the milk from the heat, take out the vanilla pod and stir in the gelatine leaves. Pour the milk over the egg mixture, stirring carefully all the time. Pour it all back into a saucepan and let the mixture thicken while stirring it with a wooden spoon. Before the mixture comes to the boil and as it starts to thicken nicely, remove the pan from the heat. Set aside to cool.

Whisk the egg whites with 1 pinch of salt until very firm and when ready, add the powdered gelatine diluted in a little water.

Fold the egg whites into the egg mixture and let it set in a cool place for 1 hour, then spread this mousse over one cake half. Place the other cake half on top.

Gingerbread
Pain d'épice

PHASE 2
PP

- **6 to 8 servings**
- **Preparation time**
  10 minutes
- **Cooking time**
  45 minutes
- **Ingredients**
  12 tablespoons oat bran
  2 tablespoons powdered skimmed milk
  2 teaspoons baking powder
  6 tablespoons fat-free fromage frais
  3 eggs + 3 egg whites
  2 tablespoons gingerbread spice mix (cinnamon, aniseed, nutmeg, ginger, cloves)
  2 tablespoons liquid sweetener
  1 teaspoon oil (tolerated)

Preheat the oven to 180°C/350°F/Gas 4.

In a bowl, combine the bran, powdered milk and baking powder. Add the fromage frais and stir thoroughly, then add the eggs and 3 egg whites. Keep stirring until the mixture is even and smooth, then work in the spices and sweetener. Pour this mixture into an ovenproof dish or tin that has been oiled using some kitchen paper.

Bake in the oven for 45 minutes. To check whether the cake is ready, insert the end of a knife and it should come out clean.

In the Attack and Cruise phases, remember you should not eat more than 2 tablespoonfuls of oat bran per day.

Fromage frais clementine creams

Crèmes au fromage frais

PHASE 2
PP

- **6 servings**
- **Preparation time**
  20 minutes
- **Cooking time**
  30 minutes
- **Refrigeration time**
  5 hours
- **Ingredients**
  6 gelatine leaves
  2 vanilla pods
  1 litre (1¾ pints) skimmed milk
  2 clementines, satsumas or
  tangerines (unwaxed if possible)
  1 teaspoon ground cinnamon
  4 egg yolks
  4 tablespoons sweetener
  (or more according to taste)
  200g (7oz) fat-free fromage frais
  100ml (3½fl oz) crème fraîche (3%
  fat) (tolerated and optional)
  1 tablespoon clementine flavouring
  (optional)
  www.mydukandietshop.co.uk
  1 teaspoon orange flavouring
  (optional)
  www.mydukandietshop.co.uk

Leave the gelatine leaves to soak for 5 minutes in cold water.

Split the vanilla pods, scrape out the seeds and place in a pan with the milk, zest from the clementines and cinnamon. Bring to the boil and then leave to infuse for 20 minutes.

In a large bowl, whisk together the egg yolks with the powdered sweetener, fromage frais, crème fraîche and flavourings.

Using a small conical strainer, pour the milk over the egg yolks, discarding the pods, and stir together vigorously. Warm this mixture in a pan over a gentle heat, stirring continuously with a wooden spatula until the cream is thick enough to coat the back of the spatula.

Remove from the heat and stir the gelatine into the hot milk. Pour the mixture into six dishes. Leave to cool down to room temperature, then refrigerate for 5 hours.

Serve plain in the Attack and Cruise phases or with clementine segments in the Consolidation phase.

As a variation, use pistachio flavouring with the zest from a large lemon.

Grand Marnier Swiss roll

Petits roulés à la crème Grand Marnier

- **6 servings**
- **Preparation time**
  15 minutes
- **Cooking time**
  25 minutes
- **Refrigeration time**
  2 hours
- **Ingredients**
  2 gelatine leaves
  250ml (9fl oz) skimmed milk
  2 egg yolks
  1 tablespoon sweetener
  1 tablespoon cornflour (tolerated)
  1 teaspoon Grand Marnier flavouring
  (optional), orange flower water or
  some orange zest
  www.mydukandietshop.co.uk

For the sponge
  3 eggs
  3 tablespoons oat bran
  1 tablespoon skimmed milk powder
  30g (1oz) virtually fat-free quark
  30g (1oz) fat-free fromage frais
  1 tablespoon cornflour (tolerated)
  1 teaspoon baking powder
  1 teaspoon vanilla flavouring
  www.mydukandietshop.co.uk
  2 tablespoons sweetener
  Powdered sweetener (for decoration)

Leave the gelatine leaves to soak for 5 minutes in cold water.

Boil the milk. Mix together the egg yolks, powdered sweetener, cornflour and flavouring in a bowl. Remove the milk from the heat and add the gelatine to it. Stir thoroughly. Carefully pour the milk over the egg mixture, stirring continuously with a wooden spoon. Pour it all back into a saucepan and let it thicken. Leave to cool down to room temperature, then refrigerate for 2 hours.

While the cream is chilling, you can start to make the sponge. Preheat the oven to 160°C/325°F/Gas 3. Separate the egg yolks from the whites. Put the egg yolks in a bowl and stir in the bran, milk, quark, fromage frais, cornflour, baking powder, flavouring and powdered sweetener. Whisk all these ingredients together vigorously. Fold in the beaten egg whites. Spread out the sponge mixture on a silicone Swiss roll tray (turning out the sponge is easier with silicone). Bake until the sponge turns nicely golden brown. Turn the sponge out onto a damp tea towel and immediately roll it up. Leave it to cool down, then unroll the sponge. Spread the cream out over the sponge and very gently roll it up again.

In the Consolidation phase, you could spread a little strawberry coulis (see page 246) or apricot jam (see page 248) on the sponge before rolling up with the cream.

When ready to serve, dust with a little powdered sweetener.

In the Attack and Cruise phases, remember you should not eat more than 2 tablespoonfuls of oat bran per day.

Rhubarb compote

Compote de rhubarbe

- **6 servings**
- **Preparation time**
  10 minutes
- **Resting time**
  15 minutes
- **Cooking time**
  30 minutes
- **Ingredients**
  1kg (2¼lb) rhubarb
  6 tablespoons sweetener (or more according to taste)
  20 drops of vanilla flavouring or another flavour (depending on the flavouring, try adding 10 drops, taste and add more if required)
  www.mydukandietshop.co.uk

Quickly wash the rhubarb and without peeling it chop it up into 1-2cm (½-¾ inch) thick chunks.

Put the rhubarb chunks in a colander and sprinkle over the sweetener. Let the rhubarb drain for 10 to 15 minutes, reserving the rhubarb liquid.

Cook over a gentle heat in its own liquid, taking care to stir at regular intervals. Leave to simmer away like this for about thirty minutes, until you have the consistency you want. Once cooked, add the flavouring, leave to cool a little then purée the compote.

Lemon and lime mousses

Verrines de mousse aux deux citrons

PHASE 3

- **6 servings**
- **Preparation time**
  25 minutes
- **Cooking time**
  35 minutes
- **Refrigeration time**
  2 hours 30 minutes
- **Ingredients**
  For the candied fruit
  4 tablespoons sweetener
  1 unwaxed lemon
  1 unwaxed lime
  For the mousse
  2 unwaxed lemons
  2 gelatine leaves
  4 eggs
  3 tablespoons sweetener
  150ml (5fl oz) skimmed milk
  1 pinch of salt

For the candied fruit, combine the powdered sweetener with 50ml (2fl oz) water, warm over a gentle heat and put to one side.

Cut the lemon and lime into very thin slices and remove any pips. Cut the slices into quarters. Boil them in the syrup over a gentle heat for almost 20 minutes. Leave to cool, then strain. Put these pieces of candied lemon and lime to one side to decorate the mousses later on. Keep 2 tablespoons of syrup for the mousses.

To make the mousses, start by grating the lemon zest, then put the zest to one side in a small dish. Squeeze the juice and put it to one side too.

Leave the gelatine leaves to soak for 5 minutes in cold water.

Whisk 2 eggs and 2 egg yolks with the powdered sweetener until the mixture turns frothy (put the egg whites to one side). Add the zest and lemon juice, put the mixture into a saucepan and let it thicken a little over a gentle heat. Pour in the milk very gradually. Remove the pan from the heat and work in the gelatine.

Whisk the egg whites with the pinch of salt until firm. When almost finished, gently fold in the 2 tablespoons of syrup, then work this into the lemon mixture.

Cover with a layer of mousse and decorate with some candied lemon and lime on top. Refrigerate the mousses for at least 2½ hours before serving.

PHASE 3

Vanilla-hazelnut crème brûlée with strawberries

Crème brûlée vanille-noisette, petits dés de fraise

- **6 servings**
- **Preparation time**
  15 minutes
- **Cooking time**
  40 minutes
- **Refrigeration time**
  1 hour
- **Ingredients**
  500ml (18fl oz) skimmed milk
  1 vanilla pod
  4 egg yolks
  6 tablespoons sweetener
  ½ teaspoon hazelnut flavouring
  (optional)
  www.mydukandietshop.co.uk
  12 strawberries
  200ml (7fl oz) crème fraîche
  (3% fat) (tolerated)

Pour the skimmed milk into a saucepan, split the vanilla pod in half, scrape out the seeds and add to the milk. Bring to the boil. Leave to infuse for 5 to 10 minutes and then remove the vanilla pod.

Preheat the oven to 180°C/350°F/Gas 4.

Separate the eggs and in a large bowl, beat the egg yolks with the powdered sweetener and hazelnut flavouring.

Cut the strawberries into small pieces and arrange them in six large ramekins or dishes.

Stir the hot milk thoroughly into the egg yolks and then add the crème fraîche. Pour this mixture over the strawberries and bake in the oven for 30 minutes.

Leave the brûlées to cool to room temperature, then place in the refrigerator for 1 hour before serving.

Lemony mousse

Mousse pulp au citron

- **6 servings**
- **Preparation time**
  15 minutes
- **Cooking time**
  20 minutes
- **Refrigeration time**
  30 minutes
- **Ingredients**
  3 unwaxed lemons
  3 eggs
  3 tablespoons sweetener (or more according to taste)
  3 tablespoons cornflour (tolerated)
  500ml (18fl oz) skimmed milk

Remove the zest from one of the lemons. Squeeze all three lemons.

Put the lemon zest and juice in a saucepan and add the egg yolks and powdered sweetener. Combine these ingredients thoroughly, then stir in the cornflour, mixing it in gradually.

Heat the mixture up, stirring all the time with a wooden spoon. Let it thicken and then add the skimmed milk, little by little. Stir well and let it thicken some more. Remove from the heat and leave to cool down.

Whisk the egg whites until very firm and gently fold them into the lemon mixture. Pour this into six glasses or ramekins and refrigerate for 30 minutes before serving.

Pineapple with iced crème anglaise

Ananas et sa crème anglaise glacée

PHASE 3

- **2 servings**
- **Preparation time**
  15 minutes
- **Cooking time**
  20 minutes
- **Freezing time**
  3 hours
- **Ingredients**
  1 vanilla pod
  200ml (7fl oz) skimmed milk
  3 egg yolks
  3 tablespoons sweetener
  20 drops of white rum flavouring
  (optional)
  www.mydukandietshop.co.uk
  2 large slices of pineapple, cut in half

Split the vanilla pod, scrape out the seeds and place in a pan with the milk. Bring to the boil. Remove from the heat and take out the vanilla pod.

In a large bowl, whisk together the egg yolks with the powdered sweetener and white rum flavouring. Pour the hot milk over the egg yolks, stirring vigorously. Warm this mixture over a gentle heat, stirring continuously with a wooden spatula until the cream covers the back of the spatula. Pour the mixture into two glasses.

Leave to cool to room temperature and then place in the freezer for 3 hours.

When you are ready to serve the dessert, take the creams out of the freezer and present them on a plate with the pineapple slices.

Apricot clafoutis

PHASE 3

Clafoutis pistache-abricot

- **6 servings**
- **Preparation time**
  10 minutes
- **Cooking time**
  45 minutes
- **Ingredients**
  4 eggs
  30g (1 oz) wholemeal flour
  400ml (14fl oz) skimmed milk
  3 tablespoons sweetener
  1 teaspoon baking powder
  2 tablespoons pistachio flavouring
  (optional)
  www.mydukandietshop.co.uk
  14 ripe apricots

Preheat the oven to 180°C/350°F/Gas 4.

Beat the eggs, then beat in the flour, milk, sweetener, baking powder and flavouring.

Halve the apricots, remove the stones and arrange the halves in rows in one non-stick dish or six small dishes. Cover with the egg mixture.

Bake in the oven for 45 minutes. Check to see if the clafoutis is ready and, if necessary, leave it in the oven a little longer.

Take the clafoutis out of the oven and let it cool down before you eat it.

Spicy compote

Compote aux épices

PHASE 3

- **4 servings**
- **Preparation time**
  25 minutes
- **Cooking time**
  30 minutes
- **Ingredients**
  1 orange
  1kg (2¼lb) apples
  1 cinnamon stick
  1 clove
  3 tablespoons oat bran
  2 cardamom pods

Peel the orange and cut it into quarters.

Peel the apples and then cut them into small cubes.

Lightly toast the cinnamon, clove, oat bran and seeds from the cardamom pods in a clean non-stick frying pan, then add the orange and apple.

Cook with the lid on over a medium heat for about 30 minutes until the apples start to break down.

Sprinkle with oats and serve.

Vanilla panna cotta with raspberries and balsamic syrup

PHASE 3

Panacotta vanille, sirop balsamique et petites framboises

- **4 servings**
- **Preparation time**
  15 minutes
- **Cooking time**
  20 minutes
- **Refrigeration time**
  8 hours
- **Ingredients**
  4 gelatine leaves
  2 vanilla pods
  500ml (18fl oz) skimmed milk
  4 egg yolks
  4 tablespoons sweetener
  200ml (7fl oz) crème fraîche (3% fat)
  (tolerated)
  A drizzle of balsamic vinegar syrup,
  bought or made by reducing down
  balsamic vingear until thickened (the
  smell is very strong so ventilate the
  kitchen well)
  20 raspberries (or more if you really
  enjoy them)

Leave the gelatine leaves to soak for 5 minutes in cold water.

Split the vanilla pods, scrape out the seeds and place in a pan with the milk. Bring the milk to the boil.

In a bowl, whisk together the egg yolks with 2 tablespoons of the powdered sweetener.

Remove the vanilla pods and pour the milk over the egg yolks, stirring continuously. Put the mixture back in the pan and warm over a gentle heat, stirring all the time with a wooden spatula, until the cream is thick enough to coat the spatula.

Remove from the heat and stir in the gelatine. Leave to cool to room temperature.

In a bowl, whisk together the crème fraîche and remaining sweetener, then add the egg mixture. Pour this into four small moulds or ramekins and leave to rest until at room temperature. Refrigerate for 8 hours.

When ready to serve, turn the panna cottas carefully out onto plates, add a trickle of the balsamic vinegar syrup and decorate with the raspberries.

Strawberry and vanilla puddings

Soja entre deux fraises

- **2 servings**
- **Preparation time**
  10 minutes
- **Refrigeration time**
  10 minutes
- **Ingredients**
  100g (3½oz) strawberries
  ½ lemon
  Sweetener (according to taste)
  300g (10½oz) vanilla-flavoured soya
  yoghurt or plain soya yoghurt with
  vanilla sweetener

Hull the strawberries and purée with the juice of half a lemon and the sweetener. Taste, add more sweetener if necessary, and refrigerate for 10 minutes.

Pour some of the strawberry coulis into two glasses. Add a layer of yoghurt, another layer of coulis, and then finish with the remaining yoghurt.

Apricot jam

Confiture d'abricot

- **Makes 1 jar**
- **Preparation time**
  15 minutes
- **Cooking time**
  15 minutes
- **Ingredients**
  300g (10½oz) ripe apricots
  4 tablespoons sweetener
  (more or less according to taste)
  A little ground cinnamon
  ½ teaspoon agar-agar

Wash the apricots, cut into quarters and remove the stones. Put them in a pan with the sweetener and ground cinnamon. Bring to the boil, turn down the heat and leave to simmer for 5 minutes.

Add the agar-agar and cook for 1 minute over a gentle heat, stirring well. Gently mash the mixture with a fork.

Pour the mixture straightaway into a sterilized jar, seal using some clingfilm and a rubber band, then seal with the lid. Store in a cool place.

Floating islands with a hint of mocha

Îles flottantes note moka

PHASE 3

- **4 servings**
- **Preparation time**
  15 minutes
- **Cooking time**
  20 minutes
- **Refrigeration time**
  1 hour
- **Ingredients**
  1 vanilla pod or 1 teaspoon vanilla
  flavouring
  www.mydukandietshop.co.uk
  375ml (13fl oz) light evaporated milk
  (4% fat)
  100ml (3½fl oz) skimmed milk
  4 eggs
  1 teaspoon mocha coffee flavouring
  (optional) or very strong coffee
  www.mydukandietshop.co.uk
  4 tablespoons sweetener
  1 to 2 teaspoons cornflour (tolerated)

Split the vanilla pod, if using, scrape out the seeds and place in a pan with the evaporated and skimmed milk. Bring the milk to the boil. Remove from the heat and take out the vanilla pod.

Separate the egg yolks from the whites. In a bowl, whisk the egg whites until firm with the coffee flavouring and 2 tablespoons of the powdered sweetener.

Using a tablespoon, shape the egg white into little meringues and put them in a microwave oven for 1 minute (power 800w/900w). Place the cooked meringues on some kitchen paper and leave to cool to room temperature.

In a large bowl, mix together the egg yolks with the remaining sweetener and cornflour. Gradually pour in the hot milk and then return the mixture to the pan and heat over a gentle heat. Keep stirring until the cream is thick enough to coat the back of the spoon. Leave to cool down to room temperature and then place in the refrigerator for 1 hour.

Pour the cream into four dessert dishes, then arrange the meringues on top.

Cinnamon apple surprise

Pommes surprise à la cannelle

- **4 servings**
- **Preparation time**
  15 minutes
- **Cooking time**
  25 minutes
- **Ingredients**
  4 large Golden Delicious apples
  1 egg
  200g (7oz) virtually fat-free cottage cheese
  2 tablespoons sweetener
  1 teaspoon ground cinnamon
  1 teaspoon vanilla essence

Preheat your oven to 180°C/350°F/Gas 4.

Core and cut the top off each apple. Scoop out some of the flesh without making a hole in the skin.

In a bowl, beat together the egg, drained cottage cheese, sweetener, cinnamon and vanilla essence.

Fill the apples with this mixture, put the tops back on the apples and wrap them in greaseproof paper.

Place on a baking tray and bake in the oven for 25 minutes.

Serve and eat while warm.

Index

aniseed-flavoured
veal stew with
fennel 186-7
apples
chicken, apple
and vegetable
curry 204-5
cinnamon apple
surprise 252-3
spicy compote
242-3
apricots
apricot clafoutis
240-1
apricot jam 248-9
Asian-style mussels
184-5
asparagus
chicken and
prawns in a spicy
coconut sauce
210-11
lobster with eggs
and smoked
salmon 148
aubergines
aubergine and
tofu lasagne
198-9
baked vegetable
terrine 149
chicken, apple
and vegetable
curry 204-5

baked vegetable
terrine 149
basil, red mullet
fillets with 202-3
beef
chilli con carne
with tofu 196-7
stir-fried beef with
sweet peppers
200-1
bread, Dukan
sandwich 194
bresaola
summer cocktail
topped with
bresaola 166-7
broccoli
salmon and
broccoli mousse
150-1
summer seafood
surprise 160-1
butternut squash
aniseed-flavoured
veal stew with
fennel 186-7

carrots
carrot flan 188-9
Halloween soup
156-7
summer cocktail
topped with

bresaola 166-7
cheese
aubergine and
tofu lasagne
198-9
carrot flan 188-9
curried chicken
club sandwich
194-5
mushroom and
tofu quiche 190-1
pumpkin loaf
168-9
salt cod gratin
with chanterelle
mushrooms
178-9
chicken
chicken, apple
and vegetable
curry 204-5
chicken and
prawns in a spicy
coconut sauce
210-11
coconut chicken
with French
beans and tofu
208-9
curried chicken
club sandwich
194-5
pumpkin loaf
168-9
chicory
rabbit with a
mustard sauce
and braised
chicory 182-3
chocolate
iced chocolate
soufflés 218-19
tofu choc cream
220-1
cinnamon apple
surprise 252-3
clafoutis, apricot
240-1
cockles,
Mediterranean
180-1
coconut milk
chicken and
prawns in a spicy
coconut sauce
210-11
coconut chicken
with French
beans and tofu
208-9
cod
salt cod gratin
with chanterelle
mushrooms
178-9
seafood
sauerkraut 176-7
coffee

floating islands
with a hint of
mocha 250-1
iced chocolate
soufflés 218-19
courgettes
aubergine and
tofu lasagne
198-9
baked vegetable
terrine 149
chicken, apple
and vegetable
curry 204-5
crevettes and cherry
tomatoes in a
spicy cream
146-7
cucumber
cucumber
appetizers with
red roe 152-3
salmon and
cucumber
millefeuilles
144-5
smoked salmon
and cucumber
jellies 162-3
curried chicken club
sandwich 194-5

Dukan sandwich
bread 194

eggs
lobster with eggs
and smoked
salmon 148
scrambled eggs
with salmon roe
134-5
spicy omelette
with fresh mint
172-3

fennel
aniseed-flavoured
veal stew with
fennel 186-7
Halloween soup
156-7
floating islands with
a hint of mocha
250-1
fluffy pistachio
mousses 216-17
French beans
coconut chicken
with French
beans and tofu
208-9
fromage frais
clementine
creams 226-7

gingerbread 224-5
ginger, sweet

pepper soup with
164-5
Grand Marnier Swiss
roll 228-9

Halloween soup
156-7
ham mousse with
tomato sauce
158-9
hazelnuts
vanilla-hazelnut
crème brûlée
with strawberries
234-5
Hokkaido squashes
squashes
filled with veal
Bolognese 192-3

ice cream, muesli
214-15
iced chocolate
soufflés 218-19
iced crème anglaise,
pineapple with
238-9

jam, apricot 248-9
jellies
smoked salmon
and cucumber
162-3

lasagne
aubergine and
tofu lasagne
198-9
leeks
light leek mousse
with a tomato
coulis 154-5
lemons
lemon and lime
mousses 232-3
lemony mousse
236-7
light leek mousse
with a tomato
coulis 154-5
lime
lemon and lime
mousses 232-3
ling
seafood
sauerkraut 176-7
lobster with eggs
and smoked
salmon 148

medallions of sole
with salmon
174-5
Mediterranean
cockles 180-1
meringues
floating islands
with a hint of

mocha 250-1
millefeuilles, salmon
and cucumber
144-5
mini smoked salmon
vol-au-vents
132-3
mint, spicy omelette
with fresh 172-3
muesli ice cream
214-15
mushrooms
mushroom and
tofu quiche 190-1
salt cod gratin
with chanterelle
mushrooms
178-9
mussels
Asian-style
mussels 184-5
seafood
sauerkraut
176-7
smoked salmon
parcels 142-3
mustard
rabbit with a
mustard sauce
and braised
chicory 182-3

Normandy-style
coquilles
Saint-Jacques
206-7

omelette
spicy omelette
with fresh mint
172-3
orange
fromage frais
clementine
creams 226-7
Grand Marnier
Swiss roll 228-9
muesli ice cream
214-15
spicy compote
242-3

pan-fried scallops
with vanilla foam
140-1
peppers
baked vegetable
terrine 149
stir-fried beef with
sweet peppers
200-1
sweet pepper
soup with ginger
164-5
pineapple with iced
crème anglaise
238-9
pistachio mousses,

fluffy 216-17
prawns
chicken and
prawns in a spicy
coconut sauce
210-11
crevettes and
cherry tomatoes
in a spicy cream
146-7
Mediterranean
prawns in a
vanilla sauce
138-9
seafood
sauerkraut 176-7
pumpkins
Halloween soup
156-7
pumpkin loaf
168-9

rabbit with a mustard
sauce and
braised chicory
182-3
raspberries
vanilla panna
cotta with
raspberries and
balsamic syrup
244-5
red mullet
red mullet fillets
with basil 202-3
rhubarb compote
230-1
roe
cucumber
appetizers with
red roe 152-3
scrambled eggs
with salmon roe
134-5

St Tropez tart 222-3
salmon
medallions of
sole with salmon
174-5
salmon and
cucumber
millefeuilles
144-5
see also smoked
salmon
salmon and broccoli
mousse 150-1
salmon roe,
scrambled eggs
with 134-5
salt cod gratin
with chanterelle
mushrooms
178-9
sauerkraut, seafood
176-7
scallops

Normandy-style coquilles Saint-Jacques 206-7
pan-fried scallops with vanilla foam 140-1
seafood sauerkraut 176-7
seafood sticks (surimi) summer seafood surprise 160-1
smoked eel seafood sauerkraut 176-7
smoked haddock seafood sauerkraut 176-7
smoked salmon
  salmon and broccoli mousse 150-1
  lobster with eggs and smoked salmon 148
  mini smoked salmon vol-au-vents 132-3
  smoked salmon and cucumber jellies 162-3
  smoked salmon parcels 142-3
  summer seafood surprise 160-1
sole
  medallions of sole with salmon 174-5
soufflés, iced chocolate 218-19
soups
  Halloween soup 156-7
  sweet pepper soup with ginger 164-5
spicy compote 242-3
spicy omelette with fresh mint 172-3
squashes filled with veal Bolognese 192-3
stir-fried beef with sweet peppers 200-1
strawberries
  strawberry and vanilla puddings 246-7
  vanilla-hazelnut crème brûlée with strawberries 234-5
summer cocktail

topped with bresaola 166-7
summer seafood surprise 160-1
Swiss roll, Grand Marnier 228-9

tandoori tofu 136-7
tart, St Tropez 222-3
tofu
  aubergine and tofu lasagne 198-9
  chilli con carne with tofu 196-7
  coconut chicken with French beans and tofu 208-9
  mushroom and tofu quiche 190-1
  tandoori tofu 136-7
  tofu choc cream 220-1
tomatoes
  aubergine and tofu lasagne 198-9
  crevettes and cherry tomatoes in a spicy cream 146-7
  ham mousse with tomato sauce 158-9
  light leek mousse with a tomato coulis 154-5
  mushroom and tofu quiche 190-1
  Normandy-style coquilles Saint-Jacques 206-7
  red mullet fillets with basil 202-3
  summer cocktail topped with bresaola 166-7

vanilla
  cinnamon apple surprise 252-3
  floating islands with a hint of mocha 250-1
  Mediterranean prawns in a vanilla sauce 138-9
  muesli ice cream 214-15
  pan-fried scallops with vanilla foam 140-1

rhubarb compote 232-3
strawberry and vanilla puddings 246-7
vanilla-hazelnut crème brûlée with strawberries 234-5
vanilla panna cotta with raspberries and balsamic syrup 244-5
veal
  aniseed-flavoured veal stew with fennel 186-7
  squashes filled with veal Bolognese 192-3
vol-au-vents, mini smoked salmon 132-3

Acknowledgements

My thanks go to all those people who throughout my life have helped me build this method. And most of all, I would like to thank my anonymous readers and patients who, of their own volition, have quite spontaneously gone about making the method known.

And among them, there is one who stands out: Carole Kitzinger. As talented as she is able, and yet so modest. Without her, this book would never have happened. And since I am thanking people, I want to mention Vahinée, who knows my method perhaps better than I do.

Nathalie, Christine, Laetitia, Camelia and Isabelle, names to you, but for me they are stars.

First published in France in 2009 by Flammarion

First published in Great Britain in 2011 by
Hodder & Stoughton
An Hachette UK company

1

Copyright © Pierre Dukan 2011

A CIP catalogue record for this title is available from the British Library

Hardback ISBN 978 1 444 76329 4
Ebook ISBN 978 1 444 73608 3

Typeset in Helvetica LT and Din by Bobby&Co Design
Design by Alice Leroy
Photography by Bernard Radvaner

Printed and bound in China by C&C Offset Printing Co. Ltd.

Hodder & Stoughton policy is to use papers that are natural, renewable and recyclable products and made from wood grown in sustainable forests. The logging and manufacturing processes are expected to conform to the environmental regulations of the country of origin.

Hodder & Stoughton Ltd
338 Euston Road
London NW1 3BH

www.hodder.co.uk